# That's My Story, too!

From the
Killing Fields of Cambodia
to the
Healing Waters of Baptism

## Sophal Ngin

with Stephen R. Gorton

# Table of Contents

*"…for I did liken all scriptures unto us, that it might be for our profit and learning."*

1 Nephi 19:22

Sophal Ngin Family

# 1.    The Fate of P113

A salty spray of seawater from the bay off the shores of Cambodia hit my face as I stood on the edge of ship P111, waiting helplessly for news from P113. The waves below us rose like vengeful spirits, crashing against our ship with relentless force, ominous waves that rolled like dark chariots preparing for battle. A blistering sun burned overhead, its relentless rays searing down on the shimmering azure sea.

Like its sister ships, P111 and P112, Cambodian Naval Ship P113 was an old French ship built for a crew of 28 men, with officers' quarters, a galley canteen, and two heads belowdecks. But on that April morning in 1975, the landing craft rode low and slow, weighed down by more than three hundred people escaping the Khmer Rouge and their murderous overthrow of Cambodia.

Chan Chrisna, captain of P111, kept his eyes fixed on the radio transceiver. The communication channel crackled as he attempted to establish contact with the captain of P113.

"P113, do you read me?" Captain Chrisna's voice rose above the noisy hum of the antiquated French engines.

No response.

Chan Chrisna was a captain in the Royal Khmer Navy. Established in 1954, the navy patrolled Cambodia's maritime coastline and territorial waters, monitoring its deep-water ports and major waterways. The Royal Khmer Navy was formed with an initial strength of just 600 men under the authority of Captain Pierre Coedes, a naval officer acting as Chief of Naval Operations. He commanded a handful of World War II ex-French Navy vessels transferred to Cambodia at the end of the First Indochina War.

By 1970, the Royal Khmer Navy, re-designated the Khmer National Navy, stood at about 1,600 seamen under the command of Rear Admiral Vong Sarendy, who manned two fleets and a training squadron. The Cambodian Navy was responsible for escorting supply convoys on the lower Mekong-Bassac corridors. Such operations were carried out in conjunction with the Khmer Air Force, which provided air cover to these naval operations with Douglas AC-47D Spooky gunships and Helio AU-24 Stallion mini-gunships. By January 1972, the Khmer National Navy had expanded to 5,500 men, including 430 officers. I was one of those men.

As the Khmer Rouge, the Communist Party of Kampuchea, or CPK, steadily advanced towards the capital city of Phnom Penh, a palpable tension swept over the Naval Base where our ships were harbored. Hastening their retreat, American forces withdrew from the impending danger. Amidst this chaos, our three vessels were deployed with the critical mission of safeguarding the bay surrounding the naval base.

Our first directive, however, was to evacuate our families and friends—parents, children, siblings, grandparents, anyone living on or near the base—and move them to an island about 20 miles from mainland

Cambodia. We scrambled to gather everyone together. Each ship left for the island carrying about 300 people. Once the passengers were secured and safe on that island refuge, the three ships could then return to protect the bay.

Before reaching the island, a battle of our own erupted on board the ships. The confrontations originated from several passengers, those with families still on the mainland, who harbored growing apprehension that the crew had no plans to return to the bay. Angry cries echoed throughout the three ships as people demanded an immediate return to base.

The three vessels drew up to one another in a planned formation. Determined to mollify the edgy passengers, the captains reached an agreement: P113 would launch a passage back home. It was deemed that any passenger wishing to terminate their journey to the island could board this vessel and return home. A gangway was extended between the ships, and around 200 people, including the crew of P113, set sail for the base. P111 and P112 would patiently await contact from P113 before determining their next course of action.

Hours passed with no word from P113.

"Come in, P113. Do you read me?" Captain Chrisna repeated.

The speakers on board his ship crackled to life abruptly.

"This is P113," a voice responded. "Go ahead."

"This is Captain Chrisna of P111. I need to speak with the captain of P113."

"P111, return to base immediately," the gruff voice ordered. The authoritative urgency in the command was undisguised, almost tangible, but caught within the rhythm of static radio interference lurked a sinister back note—an unmistakable sound that chilled Captain Chrisna's spine—the bursting rattle of gunfire from automatic weapons.

"Yessir," responded Captain Chrisna. "May I speak with the captain of P113 first, sir?"

"That's not possible, Captain Chrisna," insisted the voice on the radio. "I am ordering you to return to base immediately." With the issuing of the deadly command, the calamitous eruption of gunfire continued—an ominous symphony playing out across the radio waves between the two ships. The once serene air became punctuated by the sharp, vicious staccato of bullets flying—the frightening music to a macabre soundtrack that unraveled through the ship's speakers as pure torment and despair.

"Sir, I must speak with the captain."

"You must do one thing and one thing only, Captain Chrisna; you must return to base immediately. Am I making myself clear, Captain?"

Heart-wrenching cries for mercy echoed off the cold steel walls of P113, hauntingly pulsating over staticky radio waves. The captain listened to the frantic pleas and piercing cries that bellowed above the blast of gunfire. The desperate appeals of the people on board P113 were fading echoes highlighting an impending doom. All two hundred people aboard P113 were being slaughtered.

The Khmer Rouge had turned the vessel into a floating tomb for the terror-stricken sailors and innocent citizens. Captain Chrisna turned his attention toward me.

"Let the crew know we cannot go back, Sergeant Ngin," Captain Chrisna told me. "If we do, we will all be killed."

By the end of 1975, seventy percent of the Khmer National Navy's sailors had been killed or wounded in action. The remainder—ranging from petty officers, enlisted personnel, clerical staff, divers, SEALs and commandos—had no other choice but to surrender and were subsequently shot to death by Khmer Rouge firing squads. Their bodies were dumped into shallow graves dug in forests near the naval facilities. Naval officers were also executed, including Rear Admiral Vong Sarendy, who missed several opportunities to leave Cambodia and was reportedly arrested and killed while trying to escape the day the capital city of Phnom Penh fell.

As I reflect on the chapters of my life, an entire array of emotions fills my heart, but one feeling persists above all else; a deep and powerful sense of gratitude toward the kind and benevolent God of Heaven who has been my protector and guiding light throughout my life.

His invisible hand has safeguarded me along my journey, allowing me to emerge from every hardship whole and mostly unharmed. This reflection gives me an overwhelming sense of wonderment and awe.

His grace has granted me the opportunity not just to live out my days but to share my extraordinary story with others. My life experiences testify to God's insurmountable might and unending compassion. I am forever indebted to Him for His benevolence in preserving my life to be shared as a beacon of inspired faith.

# 2.    Pigs, Dragons<br>& Sugar Sandwiches

I was born in Phnom Penh, Cambodia, on March 7, 1946, one year after World War II, the end of the Great War, the War to End All Wars. As I took my first breaths, the echoes of the Great War and its colossal repercussions resounded worldwide.

San Ngin Family

My father's name was San Ngin, and my mother was Sath Mom. My father's birth year symbolically embodies the essence of the pig, while my mother's birth year is associated with the mighty dragon.

Like my dad, I entered this world under the influence of the pig, a symbol of warmth, kindness, loyalty, honesty, and tenderness. Dragons, like my mother, exude decisiveness, inspiration, sensitivity, ambition, and romance—qualities that ignite passion and fuel ambition.

Cambodia is an enchanting land with breathtaking landscapes steeped in a tapestry of vibrant culture, age-old traditions, and deep-

rooted spirituality. I grew up in Phnom Penh, Cambodia's capital and most populous city. As in all of Cambodia, the widespread poverty of this capital city can still be seen. Unfortunately, today, one of the main tourist attractions for Phnom Penh is the Killing Fields of the Seventy's.

The beauty that made Phnom Penh a 'Paris of the East' and 'the Pearl of Asia' before 1970 is primarily hidden beneath the reality of modern-day Cambodia, although a few French colonial buildings remain. The wide boulevards and promenades envisaged by the French are used mainly as parking spaces and market stalls. The Khmer temples and monuments are some of the most stunning examples of Buddhist architecture and art.

Phnom Penh has three distinct seasons: the cold season, the warm season, and the relentless rainy season. To tourists exploring Phnom Penh, these seasons present themselves as Hot, Too Hot, and Too Hot and Humid—a ruthless and unremitting combination of sweltering temperatures and oppressive rains envelop visitors in a sultry embrace of perspiration.

Life in Cambodia was a relentless struggle. I was the oldest of six children, three boys and three girls. We were destitute, struggling to make ends meet, and food was scarce—so scarce, in fact, that my mother grew weak and frail. At times, we had only two eggs to feed eight people.

Battling malnourishment and succumbing to illness left her unable to breastfeed her precious infants. Consequently, two of her children fell gravely ill, their frail bodies ravaged by sickness. At that time, we could not bear the substantial cost of a medical doctor. As a result, I tragically witnessed the untimely deaths of my cherished brother, Sophorn, and my beloved sister, Sokhorn, as they succumbed to the unyielding, obstinate grip of disease.

My parents grappled to sustain our household. As the eldest among my siblings, I shouldered a significant responsibility in alleviating our family's hardships. My parents taught me to watch over and care for my little brother, Sophon, and my two younger sisters.

"You are the oldest, Sophal," they would tell me. "You must keep an eye on your brother and sisters. When they need something, you must do what they want. You help them."

Cambodia's scorching heat and stifling humidity relentlessly push its people to awaken at the break of dawn. My mother would rouse me around five o'clock in the morning. I certainly didn't want to get up that early. I was

tired, but she was insistent. I would help my mother make breakfast for our family, and that is where I began to acquire the culinary skills I would come to use later in life.

Before heading to school, I would walk to a local bakery about a mile away and buy bread to sell in the streets. I purchased two dozen loaves for eight riels and would sell them for one riel each or a half loaf for half a riel. I also brought sugar and brown sugar in cans in my bag. After purchasing the bread, I would start back toward my home, yelling, "Fresh Bread! Fresh Bread! Get your fresh bread here."

Customers off the street would call out, "Hey, boy, c'mere." I would slice the bread open for them, then sprinkle the inside with sugar or brown sugar. It was like a sugar sandwich.

Sometimes, I sold all my loaves; other times, I had a few left over. If there were leftovers, we could eat them.

By seven o'clock, I had to be ready for school. When I went to kindergarten, my father would put me on his bicycle, drop me off at school, and then go to work. He was a carpenter who built homes or worked on office buildings. He even helped create a *wat*—a Buddhist or Hindu temple in Cambodia. *Wat* is a Thai word taken from Sanskrit, meaning 'enclosure'. Later, he worked as a carpenter in the Naval Shipyards near Kampong Som. I had to walk to school when I began attending the upper levels.

My father encouraged my studies, always motivating and inspiring me to strive for excellence in my education.

"Look at how poorly our family lives," he told me. "You need to study hard, listen to your teachers, don't fool around at school. Pay attention to what your teachers are telling you. You must do better in life."

His continuous support boosted my confidence. He motivated me during challenging times, reminding me that hard work, perseverance, and dedication are critical ingredients for success. Thanks to him, I learned to value education as an essential tool for personal growth and development. My father's belief in me drove me to push myself academically and achieve all I have accomplished.

My mother would cook food to sell in the market and on the sidewalks in Phnom Penh day and night. She would take me to the market with her. She taught me the various ingredients required to make meals and what dishes we should prepare to sell. My mother taught me to cook soup, rice, noodles, and barbeque. I learned a lot from her; eventually, it all paid off when I became a professional chef.

We studied our three R's in school—writing, reading, and arithmetic. We had to pass tests in each subject to qualify for college. The Cambodian government provided some support toward higher education, but it covered only forty percent of our college tuition. My parents were too poor to support my further education, and I took a part-time job in construction. I worked eight hours a day but still struggled to meet my expenses. Food and clothing were expensive, and I had to pay my college tuition fees.

# 3.    A Steamboat Adventure

From a young age, the passion for art engulfed me. I found solace and excitement in creating beautiful artwork that evoked emotion and told stories. With time, this love for art led me to dream of becoming an architect, as the field perfectly blended my artistic inclination with my desire to create functional structures.

However, as I delved deeper into my academic journey, I realized that my skills in mathematics were not on par with the requirements for architecture. Numbers and formulas seemed to elude me. The disappointment I felt was overwhelming—to be so enamored by a profession but hindered by a lack of mathematical prowess was disheartening. Still, I refused to let go of my passion for art and explored other avenues within the creative realm where math might play a lesser role.

I vividly recall the day I was first introduced to the enchanting world of Disney through the iconic cartoon *Steamboat Willy*. As a young child, I was entirely captivated by the

magical experience of seeing these ink drawings transform into lifelike characters right before my eyes.

The sight of Mickey Mouse navigating his steamboat across the screen left me amazed, unable to comprehend how these static images could suddenly burst into motion. Each frame brought forth the illusion of movement and depth, transporting me to a realm where anything seemed possible. The meticulous attention to detail in every stroke intrigued me immensely. From Mickey's fluid movements to his playful interactions with other animated figures, it was like an entire universe had been created on that flickering screen.

Walt Disney demonstrated an unrivaled ability to evoke emotion through visuals alone. These seemingly simple cartoons transported me into a world of joy, laughter, and occasional tears. Whether it was Mickey's mischievous antics or his heartfelt expressions of love and friendship, each scene left an indelible mark on my young heart.

*Steamboat Willy* served as a gateway into discovering an ever-expanding universe of Disney masterpieces. I shifted my focus towards graphic design and illustration, where mathematical concepts were generally less pronounced. These fields allowed me to channel my artistic abilities freely, and I immersed myself in various art-related activities.

Though I still yearned for architectural creation at times, finding alternative paths within the artistic sphere has been fulfilling. As an artist now specializing in design and illustration, I can utilize my talents without feeling restricted by math's imposing presence. While my architectural dreams may have diminished due to mathematical challenges, they opened doors leading me toward an equally rewarding career path that allowed me to fully embrace my love of painting.

I began making my own comic books in college, though unlike American comic books. I focused on crafting stories that resonated with Cambodians by drawing from our familiar narratives. I intended to infuse these stories with my personal touch and bring them to life through captivating illustrations. My comic book heroes emerged as formidable figures encompassing traits of immense strength and expert kung-fu skills.

With every stroke of the pen and each carefully crafted storyline, I sought to engage readers in thrilling tales that mirrored our Cambodian cultural heritage. I created characters that encapsulated the spirit of bravery and resilience admired in our society. The protagonists in my comic books possessed physical prowess and embodied moral values such as compassion, justice, and honor.

The images seemed to dance across the pages as I poured my heart into illustrating scenes showcasing intense battles between these mighty musclemen and martial arts warriors. Decades may have passed since that first encounter with *Steamboat Willy*, but its spellbinding effect remains etched in my memory.

As a child, I never could have imagined the tragedies that would unfold for me on a similar steamboat. Time and the innocence of youth shielded me from the grim realities that awaited me aboard the Khmer National Navy vessel P111 and the harrowing adventure that forever altered my world—tragic experiences taught me valuable lessons about resilience, solidarity, and the fragility of life. The haunting memories remind me of the precarious balance between safety and danger in our unpredictable existence and our ultimate dependence on our benevolent Creator.

# 4. The Cartoonist

I decided to pursue my passion for art by enrolling in a reputable four-year college art school. Excitement surged as I stepped into the world of creativity and expression. I eagerly signed up for drawing, painting, and sculpture classes—basically any art class that was available to me.

There were usually between sixteen to twenty students in each art class. My family was too poor to buy the supplies I needed for art school: rag paper, colored pencils, brushes, paints, and canvas. I had to save money from selling bread to pay for my art supplies. Our teacher would give us assignments and monthly drawing, painting, or sculpting exams. The Disney Company donated many of the art supplies at the school.

Being financially destitute, I couldn't afford my own set of quality paintbrushes. This hindrance did not deter me, however. Instead, it sparked my resourcefulness and creativity. With limited options, I ingeniously resorted to using chicken feathers as makeshift paintbrushes. It was, I admit, an unconventional choice. Yet, to this day, whenever I glance at an exquisite painting created with meticulous brushstrokes, a sense of gratitude floods over me for those humble chicken feathers that propelled me forward on my artistic journey.

It was about this time that I began creating my comic books. Unfortunately, I had no money to print my books, so I sold my original artwork to the local library. If the library liked my stories, they would purchase and print them. Writing a story took me about three months, and I would be paid 300 riels for each comic book. Sometimes, they liked my work and would buy it; other times, they didn't. In those cases, I would rewrite the stories until they did like them. It was like being given a do-over.

At one point, I was paid thirty riels for a piece of artwork I had created. I gave twenty riels to my mother, but I secretly kept ten for myself. I needed to purchase more art supplies to finish my comic book, so I lied to my parents about how much money I had been paid. I had been working on a new comic book for nearly two months when my father discovered I had held back a third of my money. He was furious with me.

In a fit of anger and frustration, my father forcefully snatched my carefully crafted work, his face twisted with rage. He stormed

out of the house, his heavy footsteps pounding across the floor and onto the street. My heart sank, knowing what would come next. As I followed him to the river's edge, panic consumed me. My father tossed my precious drawings into the river.

Desperate to salvage any remnants of my art before they were lost forever, I jumped into the water. My once pristine pages floated aimlessly around me—some partially torn or soaked beyond saving. My hands trembled as I plucked them from their watery ruins. Returning to dry land, I laid out the dampened drawings beneath the sun's warm rays, hoping to restore them.

Although disheartened at the loss, I refused to be defeated by this setback. With renewed determination, I vowed to recreate those ruined pages. I went to the library and requested an extension. They gave me one more week to complete my comic book.

Days turned into nights as sleep was sacrificed for countless hours, striving to resurrect what was lost. Finally, perseverance prevailed over adversity, my creations bloomed anew, and I was paid 300 riels.

My father was grateful I had still earned the 300 riels but complained that three months was too long to work for such a small amount of money.

Our teacher shared some exciting news with us one morning in art school. An opportunity was presented for one of us to showcase our artistic skills and draw for the local newspaper. The newspaper had specific guidelines on the type of picture they were looking for, and each student eagerly picked up their pencils to create their own interpretation.

As I embarked on this artistic challenge, I couldn't help but feel a mix of nerves and enthusiasm. I carefully began sketching my vision with graphite on the crisp white paper before me. As the minutes ticked away, my classmates hunched over their desks, deep in concentration, as they brought their artwork to life.

Our teacher collected all the drawings and sent them off to the newspaper. Impatience gnawed at our hearts as we awaited the verdict determining whose artwork would grace the pages of our local publication. Finally, the day arrived when our teacher walked into class holding a letter from the newspaper. My heart raced with anticipation as he read aloud the four names of those who had made it into consideration for publication. Fortunately, my name was among those talented individuals—I was the fourth-best student in class!

Independent magazines hired the first three students to do illustrations. I was offered a job with the newspaper.

My teacher asked if I was alright with that.

"It's not good money, Sophal," he told me. "But it could still be good for you."

Although I didn't claim first place in this drawing challenge, being recognized and acknowledged by professionals was an honor that sparked a fire within me to continue nurturing my artistic talents. This small taste of success fueled my ambition and inspired me to set higher artistic goals—continuously striving towards improvement while never losing sight of a genuine passion for creativity.

So, I went to work at the press. I was given an office with an art table, pencils, pens, and ink—everything I needed to do the job. The newspaper paid me 300 riels a month, and I used 200 to cover my expenses. The other 100 riels I would give to my mom to buy food and clothing.

I was given the fantastic opportunity to create cartoons regularly, typically two or three times a week. Each time, I was tasked with designing two distinct types of cartoons: one filled with humor and wit, and another that delved into politics.

For the funny cartoons, I relied on laughter-inducing scenarios and whimsical characters to evoke joy and amusement as I attempted to bring smiles to people's faces with clever punchlines and lighthearted storytelling.

Crafting political cartoons demanded a different approach. These illustrations aimed to tackle current events, social issues, or political landscapes. Through thought-provoking visuals and symbolism, I strived to provide commentary on public interest matters while maintaining a balanced perspective.

Cambodia's internal politics were complex at the time. Elections in 1966 brought in National Assembly members who owed little or nothing to Cambodia's Prince Sihanouk. Although the prince was still a revered figure among the rural populace, he became increasingly unpopular with the educated elite. Conservatives resented his break with the United States and his seemingly pro-communist foreign policy. Cambodian radicals opposed his internal policies, which were economically conservative and intolerant of dissent. The prince believed that the radical sector was the greatest threat to his regime. Without hesitation, he began using severe measures—including imprisonment without trial, assassinations, and the burning of villages—to impose his will.

On one occasion, I was tasked with creating a satirical political cartoon to make light of the Cambodian military. The cartoon depicted a soldier underneath an old tree, aiming his gun at a bird perched on a branch directly above him. As he pulled the trigger, anxious to hit his target, fate took an ironic turn. The soldier missed the bird completely, striking the fragile branch beneath it instead. Instantly, the weakened branch snapped and plummeted toward the ground in free fall. The heavy impact of the wooden branch squarely struck the soldier on his un-helmeted head with a resounding thud, ending the poor soldier's life.

I couldn't help but wonder what impact my cartoons were having. Little did I know that my work had caught the attention of the Secret Police.

# 5.    Arrested

A month after the publication of the soldier shooting the bird cartoon, two men approached our doorstep. With a sense of trepidation, my mother answered the door and found herself face-to-face with two undercover police officers. The officers demanded to see me.

"He's not here," my mother told them. "He's working at the newspaper today."

During my time at the paper, I had a jam-packed schedule that began promptly at ten in the morning and stretched to nine o'clock at night. Although my primary role was as a cartoonist, I was also required to perform various odd jobs around the busy office. When I wasn't sketching illustrations for upcoming editions, I would lend a hand with tasks such as stacking and binding newspapers. This allowed me to stay involved and contribute to the production process beyond just creating cartoons.

Two days had passed since the Secret Police had visited my home. Anxiety lingered around me, and then a hushed silence fell over me as two stern-looking Secret Police officers entered the newspaper's offices. Without hesitation, they demanded I accompany them to the Police headquarters. Their grim expressions betrayed my hope of finding a way out of this mess. My Editor told me:

"Just go, Sophal. Go with them. Don't worry. I'll try to protect you. It's okay. You'll be alright."

"I don't know. I'm scared," I told him.

"You just do whatever they tell you. Tell them what you did. Don't lie. It'll be okay."

As I stood there, my colleagues' eyes bore into me with a mix of concern and apprehension. Thoughts raced through my mind about what could have led to this encounter. The officers remained stoic, giving no hints or explanations for their sudden arrival.

I entered the street where a Jeep and driver were waiting to take me and the two officers to the jailhouse. With each passing minute, an unsettling blend of curiosity and fear coursed through my veins. The officers provided neither explanation nor reassurance during our journey, intensifying my confusion and putting my senses on alert.

At last, we reached Police Headquarters—a foreboding symbol of authority that sent shivers down my spine. Once inside, I was escorted to a dimly lit room. Panic mingled uncomfortably with trepidation as they locked me in a cell with a couple of other inmates. One of the inmates asked:

"What are you in for?"

"I drew a cartoon making fun of the new government," I told him.

He laughed.

"Man, you're in big trouble now," he told me. "You're in huge trouble."

Time seemed to stand still as the minutes stretched on without any sign of progress or information. Vague notions abounded as wild theories materialized in my exhausted mind, seeking an explanation for my situation. Fear flitted across my consciousness like shadowy specters dancing at twilight. Uncertainty tightened its grip around me until it felt suffocating.

It felt like an eternity, but it was only a half-hour later that I was called to another room. As I cautiously entered the room, a blindingly bright light immediately assaulted my eyes. Its intensity made it impossible to discern anything beyond it, but I could vaguely sense that figures were seated on the other side of the table. The shadows shrouding their faces added an air of foreboding to their presence.

Every step closer to the source of the light seemed to amplify its intensity, causing me to squint and shield my eyes. My heart quickened its pace as both terror and apprehension danced within me.

"Who were these individuals hidden behind such an illuminating spectacle?" I asked myself. "What are they going to do to me?"

Their secret whisperings hung in the air like a delicate, ominous mist. The soft murmurings felt laden with secrets and intrigue, further heightening my anticipation. With each stride toward them, my senses intensified with a mix of trepidation.

"What's your name, man?" a voice from behind the light suddenly rang out at me.

Nervously, I managed to stammer out my response.

"Sophal Ngin," I responded, my voice betraying my anxiety.

Immediately, another question came swiftly and forcefully.

"How old are you?" the voice demanded.

Trying to keep my composure, I answered with a shaky voice.

"Twenty-one, sir."

Suddenly, the commanding voice ordered me to sit down, leaving no room for argument.

I sat down.

My heart raced as I awaited further commands or questions about my crime. The air grew tense and suffocating as silence hung heavy in the room. It was clear that my transgression carried immense weight and consequences. Fear coursed through my veins as I contemplated what would happen next. Dark thoughts, desperate and despairing, flooded my mind as an all-encompassing terror built up within me.

A loud thud reverberated through the room as a fist pounded against the table's surface.

"Do you even comprehend what you've done?" the authoritative voice resounded again.

Those words echoed ominously in my ears and sent shivers down my spine. Panic washed over me as regrets for my actions flooded back into focus. Beads of sweat formed on my forehead, and an unsettling knot twisted in my stomach. I was shaking. I wanted to scream. Fear ran through me like electricity through a wire.

The promise of protection from my Editor provided little comfort or reassurance amid this chaos. His words felt distant, unable to shield me from the imminent danger within these walls. I could feel the adrenaline coursing through my veins. The room seemed to shrink around me while anxiety expanded within like an inflated balloon on the verge of bursting.

"Yes," I stammered sheepishly. "I—I drew a cartoon. The newspaper—they assigned me to draw—."

The voice that interrupted me was piercingly loud, filled with accusation and an air of disdain.

"You didn't come up with that idea on your own?" the voice challenged harshly. Its tone cut through the room like a knife slicing through thin air. My heart skipped a beat as its words pounded in my ears.

"No!" I exclaimed, a deluge of desperation flooding my voice. "I just work for the paper," I pleaded my case as sincerely as possible. "I'm not a writer, just an illustrator."

"Why didn't you bring that drawing in for inspection before it went to publication?" the voice demanded, filled with anger and accusation.

The room seemed to hold its breath as the weight of the question lingered in the air like an unwanted presence. Flustered, I mumbled my response, barely audible.

"I don't know," I whispered.

Instantly, a clenched fist pounded on the table, sending shockwaves through the room.

"That's the law!" yelled the voice, now louder and more aggressive. "And you broke the law! Don't you realize the gravity of your actions?"

Fear crept into my veins as I struggled to find words. The threat of punishment hung heavy in the air, suffocating any hope for understanding or forgiveness. With each passing second, a profound sense of dread consumed me; this encounter carried consequences far beyond what I had ever imagined. The sudden thought of facing jail time sent shivers down my spine like an icy chill that refused to dissipate.

As I sat there, trapped within the four walls of that room, my mind grew increasingly frantic. Confused thoughts rushed through my head, each one a desperate attempt to find a glimmer of hope in this bleak situation. Countless questions plagued my racing thoughts as panic set in.

"If this happens again," the voice hollered, "You will go to jail!"

Silence engulfed the room—a silence brimming with uncertainty and fear. Then, suddenly, a ray of light entered from behind me. The door swung open, and a figure approached before me. My heart pounded with anticipation, unsure if this would be salvation or another twist in this bewildering ordeal. With cautious steps, I was led out of the room.

Leaving Police Headquarters, the fresh air felt good against my trembling skin. Conflicting emotions surged within me—relief tinged with lingering fear and gratitude mixed with apprehension. I felt a whirlwind of sensations as I took hesitant breaths, silently surveyed my surroundings, and tried to process the surreal transition from my arrest to this moment of liberation. A mix of confusion and gratitude swirled together as relief slowly washed over me.

After that incident, the newspaper's director took immediate action to prevent a similar mishap. He implemented a stringent inspection and approval process for all papers before printing.

Echoes of chaos and confusion replayed in my mind, leaving me hesitant about returning to work. It took three long weeks for my nerves to subside enough for me to find the courage to resume my duties. When I finally did return, I was still reeling from the shock of what had transpired. Eventually, my confidence began seeping back into my journalistic endeavors, and each new newspaper edition was meticulously and thoroughly vetted before publication.

# 6.    Operation Menu

In a tiny French villa outside of Paris, Henry Kissinger sat across the table from North Vietnamese representative Le Duc Tho to discuss terms for ending the Vietnam War. The two met sixty-eight times. Kissinger kept certain specific conversations secret—even from U.S. President Richard Nixon. He understood that the U.S. Congress didn't have the stomach for the Vietnam conflict and wanted the United States to withdraw without looking like it had suffered an overwhelming defeat.

I was twenty-three years old when Henry Kissinger began *Operation Menu.* A covert U.S. Strategic Air Command tactical bombing campaign conducted in eastern Cambodia, *Operation Menu* targeted sanctuaries and base areas of the People's Army of Vietnam (the North Vietnamese Army) and forces of the Viet Cong, which had used these areas for resupplying, training, and resting between campaigns across the border into South Vietnam.

The secret bombing of Cambodia continued for five years. It was a covert operation because it was an illegal operation. The United States was not at war with Cambodia. Kissinger's justification for the extensive bombing that caused immeasurable damage and brought to power the most eliminationist faction within the Khmer Rouge, which led to unfathomable genocide, was that it eliminated the enemy's safe havens. According to Henry Kissinger, it was an act of self-defense.

As Cambodians living in remote villages on the border with Vietnam, we had no idea why the United States attacked us. One day, American aircraft just started appearing overhead. We didn't understand why this happened but soon learned to fear these machines. And for years on end, we were terrorized by them.

From the onset of hostilities in South Vietnam, Cambodia's Prince Norodom Sihanouk had maintained a delicate domestic and foreign policy balancing act. Convinced of the inevitable victory of the communists in Southeast Asia and concerned for the future existence of his government, Sihanouk swung toward the left in the mid-1960s, making an agreement with Zhou Enlai of the People's Republic of China, allowing the People's Army of Vietnam and the Viet Cong to establish base areas in Cambodia and to use the port of Preah Sihanouk for the delivery of military material.

In 1967, President Lyndon B. Johnson authorized *Project Vesuvius*, a covert reconnaissance operation to obtain intelligence on the PAVN and VC base areas, hoping to change Sihanouk's political position. Under pressure from the political right at home and the US, Sihanouk agreed to more normalized relations with the Americans. He reopened diplomatic relations and formed a Government of National Salvation under pro-US General Lon Nol.

Newly inaugurated President Richard M. Nixon sought any means to withdraw from Southeast Asia and obtain "peace with honor." But while Nixon publicly favored the withdrawal of U.S. troops, he secretly escalated the Vietnam War by bombing neighboring Laos and Cambodia.

The North Vietnamese were transporting supplies and arms across the borders of their officially neutral neighbors. Nixon and Kissinger regarded bombing them as a means to pressure Hanoi. Henry Kissinger was deeply involved in the bombing raids on Cambodia—and in keeping them a secret from Congress and the public. Kissinger approved each of the 3,875 Cambodia bombing raids in 1969 and 1970 and the methods for keeping them out of the newspapers.

By the end of *Operation Menu*, the U.S. had dropped 110,000 tons of bombs, killing between 150,000 and 500,000 civilians and destabilizing the Cambodian government. The Khmer Rouge galvanized anti-American sentiment, rising to power and slaughtering three million Cambodians as part of the Cambodian genocide. There was such a displacement of Cambodians within our own country.

The Khmer Rouge used the trauma caused by these relentless U.S. attacks and tremendous quantities of bombs dropped as a recruiting tool. They convinced villagers that the only way to stop the bombings was to join their movement. Before the U.S. bombings, the Khmer Rouge was a tiny fringe movement of a few thousand. By the end of the bombings, the Khmer Rouge had grown to 200,000 soldiers. The U.S. attacks were the centerpiece of their recruiting drive. President Nixon and Henry Kissinger played a significant role in enabling the Cambodian genocide.

In October of 1973, Henry Kissinger and North Vietnamese representative Le Duc Tho were named joint recipients of the Nobel Peace Prize. Only Kissinger accepted. Tho refused the award until "peace is truly established."

A 1973 Gallup poll declared Kissinger "the most admired man in America." The acclaim, however, was short-lived. The Watergate scandal that led to Nixon's resignation revealed that Kissinger had ordered the FBI to wiretap the phones of members of the National Security Council to discover who had leaked news of the U.S. bombing of Cambodia to the press. By 1975, the communist victory in Vietnam had tarnished the legacy of Kissinger's 1973 peace efforts. On one occasion, travel documentarian Anthony Bourdain stated, "Once you've been to Cambodia, you'll never stop wanting to beat Henry Kissinger to death with your bare hands."

The Paris Peace Accords leading to a ceasefire in Vietnam were signed on January 27, 1973. To critics, "peace with honor" didn't look much different from the options available when Nixon first took power. Kissinger and Nixon wasted four years of negotiations with the Vietnamese communists, agreeing to virtually the same peace terms in 1973 that were on the table in 1969.

In total, nearly three million Vietnamese and 58,000 Americans died in Vietnam. Hundreds more are missing in action.

## 7.    The Land Mine


As the intensified conflict in Cambodia unfolded, I enlisted in the Cambodian army, specifically serving as a commando. My role within this esteemed force was to provide protection and support as an escort for one of the high-ranking generals in the Cambodian army.

The General was not an ordinary man but the blood of royalty and a confidant to the King. He held a profound affinity toward his country. He was a patriot, motivated by an unwavering love for Cambodia. Torn amid tumultuous times, the General couldn't stand idle while foreign powers threatened to rob us of our sovereignty. He was willing to fight against communism and the Khmer Rouge. He would have aligned himself with America, but after illegally bombing Cambodia and Laos, intensifying rebel forces, the Americans had left Cambodia.

The General traveled in an imposing vehicle that commanded attention. Our escort unit comprised two jeeps in front of his vehicle to ensure his safety during travels and three more stationed behind it. I joined my fellow soldiers and found my place among them as we embarked on our missions together.

We faced countless challenges—from hostile encounters with enemy forces to unpredictable circumstances that emerged unexpectedly. Yet throughout this expansive battlefront, I remained steadfast by the general's side, upholding our collective purpose with unwavering loyalty and resilience.

Day after day, I witnessed firsthand the sacrifices made by brave individuals within our ranks: their devotion resonated within every fiber of my being.

As we were escorting the general to a war zone in the countryside, chaos erupted around us. The deafening sounds of gunshots echoed through the air as helicopters circled overhead, raining down relentless firepower on both sides of the conflict. Our convoy pressed forward, navigating treacherous terrain while bullets sped past our vehicles.

The enemy's determination seemed unwavering, making it increasingly challenging for us to advance toward our destination. Despite the fierce firefight surrounding us, our unit remained resolute and committed to completing our mission.

Amidst the austerity of exploding shells and wailing sirens, as we approached the front line, our general abruptly ordered us to stop. His voice was firm and commanding, leaving no room for argument. He believed the proximity too dangerous for his convoy to continue. We swiftly brought our escort to a stop, scanning the surroundings for signs of threat or danger. A palpable tension hung heavily in the air.

As soon as we halted, I emerged from the Jeep, positioning myself next to it. The wind whisked through the open landscape. With unwavering focus, I held my weapon firmly in both hands, its weight reassuring against my palms.

Time slowed; seconds felt like eternities as I awaited the arrival of commanding orders that would dictate our next move. My heart pounded rapidly within my chest, a rhythmical reminder of the adrenaline coursing through me as the general ordered the jeeps in the rear to move to the front of the escort.

As the jeep I had been riding in began to move forward, a deafening explosion shattered the air. In an instant, chaos set in. The jeep had hit a landmine. Flames and thick plumes of smoke instantly consumed the vehicle. The terrifying blast unleashed a barrage of shrapnel, piercing through metal and tearing apart everything in its path.

Fragments of twisted metal whizzed past me with alarming speed.

The loud explosion resonated through the air, causing the ground beneath my feet to tremble violently. My heart raced in my chest as I struggled to maintain my balance, feeling an overwhelming mix of fear and adrenaline surging through my veins. Screams and cries echoed in my ringing ears as I struggled to orient myself amid the devastation. The explosion killed several soldiers. Bloodied and disoriented survivors stumbled around, frantically searching for safety.

Everywhere around us revealed glimpses of unimaginable horror—a severed bumper lying several feet away from where it should have been; shards of glass scattered haphazardly in the field; chunks of charred debris twisted into grotesque figures. Amid the wreckage lay the decapitated body of one of my comrades.

As the dust settled, I found myself standing on unsteady legs, surrounded by the chaos and devastation of this war. Suddenly, a fellow soldier appeared before me, his concerned eyes scanning my trembling form. I tried to compose myself as he spoke, his voice laced with worry.

"Are you okay, Sophal?" he asked, his gaze fixating on my right leg.

With a pang of realization, I glanced down and discovered a large shard of shrapnel embedded deep within my thigh. My physical tremors now mingled with an overwhelming surge of anguish and vulnerability. As sirens wailed in the distance and smoke filled the air above us, I desperately sought an anchor amid this sea of uncertainty. My thoughts drifted momentarily to home—to the faces of loved ones who eagerly awaited my return. As memories of home flooded my mind, overwhelming exhaustion took hold of me, and I collapsed, losing consciousness.

When awareness returned, I found myself surrounded by the busy atmosphere of a military hospital. The sharp smell of antiseptic filled the air, mingling with the distant echoes of footsteps and hushed conversations. Confusion crept in as I tried to piece together the events that led me here. I felt a dull ache throbbing throughout my body. Disoriented and weak, I turned my head to catch a glimpse of an IV drip attached to my arm, its translucent tube snaking its path toward a clear bag suspended above me. Nurses moved briskly about the room, their faces etched with concern but tinged with hope.

Unfamiliar figures passed by my bedside—other wounded soldiers seeking shelter and healing within these same sterile walls. Muffled conversations between patients merged with the low hum of medical equipment, providing a constant backdrop to my struggle. Tinted with both healing and pain, time blurred into an indistinguishable haze. Days blended into nights as nurses meticulously charted symptoms and administered medications while doctors hurriedly assessed new arrivals before disappearing behind closed doors.

As I lay in the hospital room, my mind swirled with so many emotions. The pain from my injuries was tremendous, but something else weighed heavily on my heart as well. It was a letter from my father, urging me to consider joining the Navy. He told me that city life had become increasingly dangerous and unstable.

His words resonated with me; they echoed the unease that had gripped me since my hospitalization. Perhaps it was time for a drastic change. Joining the Navy would provide me with a new purpose in life and an opportunity to escape the turmoil that had engulfed urban Cambodia.

I imagined myself standing tall on a naval ship, feeling the salty breeze against my face as I gazed at endless horizons. Away from violence and uncertainty, I could contribute to something larger than myself—defending our country while securing a safer future for those back home.

# 8.   Clackers & Snake Pits

After being discharged from the hospital, grim reality immediately descended on me. The rigid, sterile environment of the medical center abruptly shifted back to the harsh realities of war. I was immediately sent back to the front lines.

An unbroken expanse of land scarred by trenches and craters awaited me—a battlefield punctuated with the staccato of gunfire and the uneasy silences in between. I grappled again with what seemed like an endless cycle of fighting amid the grim landscape of war.

As darkness slowly started to cloak the landscape, my division was instructed to safeguard the frontline, becoming the critical resistance if any enemy advancement occurred. We became sentinel in the deathly silence of nightfall, our figures blending with shadows as we stretched across the frontline.

Beneath the persistent drizzle of cascading rain, a fellow soldier and I dug a foxhole near a sprawling palm tree. If fighting broke out, we could take cover behind the palm tree. Our military garbs were drenched, sticking to us like a second skin. With each spade of earth we shifted, we felt our safety net gradually forming beneath the exotic foliage. Still, we realized that the terrain would prove advantageous only if it remained unbreachable. So, beyond our freshly dug fortification, almost hidden within the atmospheric mist born out of relentless rain, we discreetly placed our 'Clackers,' the lethal M-18A1 Claymore mines.

The Claymore mine was an "anti-personnel fragmentation weapon" that became one of the most iconic explosive devices of post-World War II. The weapon could blast across and through waves of attacking enemy infantry in a single devastating hit—a requirement born of experience in the Pacific theater and the Korean War.

The Claymore was a "directional mine," a curved plastic pack of Composition C-3 explosives embedded with numerous steel cubes. When detonated, the mine would blast out its fragments across an arc set by the user. A command switch detonated the M18A1, an M57 firing device, squeezed three times to initiate the explosion, earning it the nickname "clacker." When detonated, approximately 700 1/8-inch steel balls blasted out at a velocity of nearly 4,000 feet per second, scything down the exposed enemy in a lethal gust.

Between the two groups securing the front line, we had placed around thirty-six "clackers." Their strategic positioning ensured that any trespassers would be greeted by an unwelcome onslaught, safeguarding us from any immediate enemy engagement.

I strained my eyes against the gloom while listening attentively for any sounds of intrusion. I knew that we were all that stood between our homeland and the Khmer Rouge, looking for an opportunity under cover of darkness. Anxiety mixed with resolve is a potent combination. Our duty was to hold until dawn arrived at any cost and not let even one enemy soldier pass.

The tense night stretched on endlessly. Time weighed heavily on the hearts of those of us huddled in our foxholes. An ominous anticipation hung in the air. It was eerily palpable. Gradually, a gentle breeze moved silently across the pitch-dark sky. The rain clouds began to disband under its quiet persistence, moving toward the horizon with obedient grace.

The departing cloud cover revealed a sky teeming with stars—billions of distant suns glowing with an intense brightness that stabbed through the depths of darkness. They were scattered haphazardly across the expansive black canvas overhead, a spectacular display mesmerizing me as I lay awake in that wet foxhole. As I gazed upward into the inky abyss overhead, a series of shooting stars began to tear across the panorama of the expansive night sky.

Each falling star seemed like an ethereal artist's brush dipped in luminescent cosmic paint, leaving radiant brushstrokes across a black canvas with countless twinkling stars. Seeing the breathtaking spectacle of celestial fireworks ignited my wonder, but I noticed I could also hear the stars fall. I heard a low hissing sound with each shooting star, like bacon sizzling in a frying pan.

Typically, a meteor burns up about sixty miles above the Earth's surface. Sound travels so much slower than light, like thunder, after the lightning flashes have disappeared. I shouldn't be able to hear the hissing of a falling star for several minutes after seeing it streak across the sky. These stars seemed to make a sound while I watched them burn up, entering our atmosphere. I learned later that these shooting stars are "electrophonic meteors' that give off very low-frequency radio waves traveling at the speed of light. The radio waves produce a sound, which I interpreted as the sizzle of a shooting star.

"Look at those stars, Sophal," my comrade said. "Can you see them!"

"Yes," I said. "I see them. They're beautiful."

"How long will this go on?" my comrade asked.

"The stars, you mean?" I said.

"No. The war. The fighting. How long before all this ends, Sophal?"

His hollow and edgy voice wavered as he spoke. I could sense the unease in every syllable he uttered. He was trying to remain strong, attempting to keep a steady speech, but the tension in his tone surged straight into my heart.

"I don't know, my friend," I quietly told him. "Maybe another year, maybe ten more years.

His fear was potent; tangible enough for me to sense him trembling at my words, but he leaned back in the foxhole and tried to relax. Within minutes he was asleep.

The air grew heavy with curiosity as I lay concealed in my foxhole, listening intently for any sign of movement. Each breath felt charged with expectation, as if something dreadful and disastrous was about to unfold. In the silence that followed, I imagined I could hear the faint reverberations of whistling that pierced the still night. It had no discernible melody or rhythm, just an elusive undertone cutting through the darkness. The sound seemed to float on the edge of my hearing, teasingly close yet just out of reach. Its faint presence added an eerie, unnerving layer to the already tense night. I strained to grasp the meaning behind the subtle sound.

Who could be out there in the shadows, creating this haunting sound? Was an enemy lurking nearby, and if so, why were they making their position known by whistling? Whatever it meant, the signal seemed to dance between reality and imagination, leaving me both entranced and unsettled.

Shortly after, I detected some activity. It was initially subtle, like a slight shudder beneath the surface of calm water. In the silence of the evening, under the dull luminescence of the moon, I detected the slightest disturbance. I focused on that spot, squinting to make out more details in the dim light. I saw it again—a rustling whisper causing oscillations within the thick vegetation. The underbrush shook gently as if brushed by a passing wind.

Something, or someone, was moving among the intertwining foliage; small branches twitched sporadically as leaves rustled. Thirty yards, twenty-five yards, twenty yards—the movement grew closer, taking the shape of a soldier crawling low and steady toward us. He carried a knife between his teeth and a rifle as he inched forward on his elbows.

I wanted to wake my comrade, but if I did, if he made any noise while waking up, he would give away our position. As the enemy moved forward, I could sense a formidable presence closing in behind him. My eyes scanned the scenario unfolding, but my sight was hindered by darkness. I could not accurately determine if he was alone or if there were more soldiers, as I imagined there would be, meticulously positioned and following his lead.

With the calculated precision of a seasoned warrior, the soldier moved in the dense underbrush like a shadow cast by an unseen source, blending seamlessly into the thick foliage. His expression was as intense as it was calm, and his eyes scanned ahead for any sign of danger or disturbance.

I laid my thumb on the M57 firing device of my clacker. The enemy soldier halted his advance as if sensing immediate danger—something was wrong.

Silently, with stealthy, fluid motion, he maneuvered his way to my left flank. His movement was strategic and essential for survival in hostile terrains. He soon became a specter hidden by green walls of vegetation, leaving behind only the ruffled leaves as a witness to his presence.

Within an ominous couple of minutes, an abrupt eruption of gunshots shattered the silence. The night swiftly turned to chaos and panic. Sleep released its grip on my friend as he snapped awake. Torn between delirium and comprehension, he blurted out, "They're coming! They're coming!" His voice resonated in the eerie darkness.

With adrenaline pumping through our veins, we clutched our weapons and sprang into action, adding to the ripples of warfare in the dead night around us.

By morning, the fighting had ceased.

As the crimson sun rose, my friend and I collected our scattered gear. The air was hot as we prepared to return to the safety of our base camp. That's when I noticed several peculiar round openings dotted across the walls of our foxhole. Curiosity got the better of me. I squeezed my eyes shut briefly, then peered carefully into one of these little earthy holes.

The sight that greeted me practically froze my heart. Mirroring my inquisitive stare was a pair of dark green eyes—ominously gleaming in the morning light. In the blink of an eye, an equally sinister forked tongue flickered in and out from beneath those mysterious eyes, followed by an almost inaudible whistle. A Russell viper, a regular on the most dangerous snake lists and responsible for most snake bites in several Asian countries, including Cambodia, looked back at me and whistled. Its menacing whistle is loud enough to scare off a potential predator.

The fear that gripped me in that moment was unlike anything I had experienced. The realization that our haven had been infiltrated made my blood run cold. I felt a paralyzing terror grip me. The feeling of vulnerability was suffocating as I realized how close we had come to disaster. The clandestine presence of these venomous predators turned our sanctuary into a perilous trap, and I grappled with the reality of sharing our foxhole with these deadly foes. The grip of fear tightened around my chest like a vice, tighter than any enemy's hands could ever have managed.

Upon returning to base, my thoughts were predominantly preoccupied with a weighty decision. In moments of solitude and reflection, my father's words about taking up a career in the Navy echoed repeatedly in my mind. Not just because he had served in the naval force himself but also due to his belief that life on land had become too precarious. I realized what I needed to do next.

I packed up my belongings and mentally prepared myself for this new journey. Though uncertain of what awaited me in the Navy, one thing was sure: life in the cities could no longer offer safety or peace. It was time for me to heed my father's call and embark on this venture towards stability and a new purpose.

Just like that, I was drafted into another unpredictable chapter of Cambodia's civil war.

# 9.    Direct Hit

I was a cook in the Navy with the rank of sergeant stationed aboard the battleship P111 under Captain Chan Chrisna. In times of battle, I was assigned as part of the chain of sailors passing ammunition to the large cannons at the front of the ship.

Our ship and two sister ships, P112 and P113, were assigned to patrol and protect

Cambodia's islands around the Bay of Kampong Som in the Gulf of Thailand.

Our most crucial responsibility was protecting the Marine commandos on any given day. The island in focus held strategic importance for the people of Cambodia. Our mission revolved around ensuring the safety of the brave marines stationed there. It was up to us to lay down an impenetrable defense shield, ready to counter and neutralize any dangers lurking on or off the island.

The sunlight reflected off the water's surface, casting shimmering patterns that glinted like diamonds. The rippling sea formed an intricate maze around us, its blue-green expanse spreading out before us. The waves rose and fell in a rhythmic dance, and a salty tang of sea air filled our nostrils. Bursts of spray erupted as our ship sliced through the waves.

Without warning, a bright trail cut through the dim light of dusk. A missile soared toward us at heart-stopping speed. With a violent splash that sent white spray jetting into air, it slammed into the water, falling short of its intended target. Within seconds, another ear-splitting sound of canon fire shattered the air. The missile rocketed towards us and made a direct hit on our vessel. The brutal impact sent shockwaves throughout the ship's entire structure. It struck into the starboard side of our ship with terrifying accuracy.

We were thrown into chaos by the force and magnitude of the strike that ripped through layers of steel like tissue paper. Alarm bells mixed with cries for help filled the ocean air. Thick, menacing clouds of black smoke billowed uncontrollably from the underbelly of our battleship, staining the once pure, blue sky with its sooty darkness. The once-gleaming hull now looked like a mangled beast, effusing us with a tangible sense of dread. Chaos loomed around us. Confusion reigned on deck. Crew members scrambled feverishly, their faces etched with fear. Desperate voices knotted together in an overwhelming disharmony of urgent requests for help.

Positioned strategically on our battleship, we swiveled our heavy artillery, aligning the guns with the distant outline of the island. A sense of dread hung in the space between heartbeats as the captain gave the order to fire. Lightning-bright streaks lit up the skyline, accompanied by thunderous blasts that punctuated the departure of each lethal projectile. The scent of metal and gunpowder filled the air around us.

Torturously slow, our ship moved away from the island toward open waters. As we gradually distanced ourselves from enemy fire, our battered vessel bobbed like a cork tossed in a churning sea. Moving out of the madness enveloping the deck, I descended below decks to assist my injured crewmates. The moment I stepped below, I was engulfed in an almost suffocating cloud of thick grey smoke.

The dimly lit insides of the vessel were punctuated by sporadic screams of pain shooting through the dense air, haunting echoes belonging to once-vigorous sailors now tragically reduced to wounded souls. The smoke-filled air echoed their desperate cries amid the constant screech of distressed metal.

Through the smoke, I caught sight of my friend, immobile and helpless within the hollow echo of the ship's walls. He lay sprawled out, his body half submerged in the rapidly filling ocean water that ruthlessly invaded the vessel. A sickening fear gripped me as I dashed toward him. Rushing water gushed around my ankles as I forced myself forward amid the chaos. I seized his arm to pull him to safety. Its burned skin tore loose in my hands.

I removed my bright orange life vest and placed it on the floor. My friend's head was drooping unnaturally. His pallid face was veiled with an eerie calmness that made reality seem spectral. Carefully, I cradled his head in my trembling hands and maneuvered it onto the makeshift pillow. The life vest morphed under his limp weight—creating an illusion of gentle sleep amidst our harsh reality. The blood oozed from his ear into my hands as his life seeped slowly from his body.

As soon as the damage was realized, the ship's maintenance crew sprang into action, diligently setting out to repair the staggering hole ripped open in the ship's side. The sharp smell of singed metal filled the air as they began welding a thick steel sheet across the gaping void, striving against time and circumstance to patch together a viable protection against the relentless sea.

In another part of the ship, the crew's medic, amid gasps and groans, worked methodically at patching up the wounded sailors as the ship's captain steered the broken vessel back toward the Naval base on the mainland. The captain made the critical decision to call in an airstrike on the isolated island.

A squadron of fighter jets from the Second World War, armed with explosives, streaked across the sky, forming a chilling silhouette against the serene skyline as they approached their target.

We reached the mainland the following morning.

# 10.  The Rise of Pol Pot

The rise of Pol Pot and the Khmer Rouge occurred in the mid-1970s. However, their path to power can be traced back to the 1960s. During this period, the Khmer Rouge functioned as the military branch of the Communist Party of Kampuchea, the name the party used for Cambodia. Their operations were mainly concentrated in northeastern Cambodia's remote jungle and mountainous regions. However, they lacked widespread backing throughout the country, especially in urban areas such as Phnom Penh.

Following a military coup in 1970, which removed Prince Norodom Sihanouk from power, the Khmer Rouge and the deposed leader formed a political coalition. Given the monarch's popularity among urban Cambodians, the Khmer Rouge gradually gained increasing support.

For the next five years, a civil war between the right-leaning military, which had led the coup, and those supporting the alliance of Prince Norodom and the Khmer Rouge raged in Cambodia. The Khmer Rouge side seized the advantage in the conflict after gaining control of increasing amounts of territory in the Cambodian countryside.

In the year 1975, Phnom Penh fell under the invasion of Khmer Rouge fighters, resulting in the capture of the city. This victory in the civil war gave the Khmer Rouge complete control over the country. Surprisingly, rather than reinstating Prince Norodom to his previous position of power, they chose to transfer authority to their leader, Pol Pot. Consequently, Prince Norodom was compelled to live in exile.

After being appointed as the head of the nation by the Khmer Rouge, Pol Pot and his loyal forces wasted no time in transforming Cambodia, which they had renamed Kampuchea, with the hopes of creating a communist-style agricultural utopia.

The Khmer Rouge began their reign with the murder of surrendering officials of the former government and the brutal emptying of the capital and other cities. Black-clad soldiers marched millions of people into the countryside and put them to work as slaves, digging canals and tending crops. Religion, popular culture, and all forms of self-expression were forbidden. Families were split apart, with children forced into mobile labor brigades. Anyone who questioned the new order risked torture and death by a blow to the head.

After declaring 1975 "Year Zero," Pol Pot isolated Kampuchea from the global community. He relocated hundreds of thousands of city dwellers to rural farming communes and abolished the country's currency. He also outlawed the ownership of private property and the practice of religion in the new nation.

Workers on the farm collectives established by Pol Pot soon began suffering from the effects of overwork and lack of food. Hundreds of thousands died from disease, starvation, or damage to their bodies sustained during back-breaking work or abuse from the ruthless Khmer Rouge guards overseeing the camps.

The regime led by Pol Pot carried out mass executions against thousands of individuals labeled as enemies of the state. Additionally, anyone identified as an intellectual or someone with the potential to lead a revolutionary movement was subject to execution. Some individuals were executed for merely appearing to be intellectuals, such as wearing glasses or being able to speak a foreign language.

As part of this effort, hundreds of thousands of educated, middle-class Cambodians were tortured and executed in special centers established in the cities. The most notorious among these was Tuol Sleng prison in Phnom Penh, where approximately 17,000 individuals, including men, women, and children, were incarcerated throughout the four-year reign of the regime.

During Pol Pot's rule of Cambodia, an estimated 2.2 million of the nation's citizens died in what later became known as the Cambodian Genocide.

Pol Pot attempted to extend his influence into the newly unified Vietnam, but his forces were quickly rebuffed. After a series of violent battles on the border between Vietnam and Cambodia in 1979, the Vietnamese Army removed Pol Pot and the Khmer Rouge from power, and Pol Pot and his Khmer Rouge fighters quickly retreated to remote areas of the country. An active insurgency remained in the country but with declining influence. Vietnam retained control through its military presence for much of the 1980s, over the objections of the United States.

In the years following the downfall of the Khmer Rouge, Cambodia has made steady progress in rebuilding its connections with the global community. However, the nation continues to grapple with significant challenges such as poverty and illiteracy. Prince Norodom assumed leadership of Cambodia in 1993, adopting a constitutional monarchy system.

Pol Pot continued to reside in the rural northeast of Cambodia until 1997, when the Khmer Rouge tried him for his crimes against the state. The trial was mostly for show, however, and the former dictator died while under house arrest in his jungle home.

The tales of anguish and suffering by the Cambodian people at the hands of Pol Pot and the Khmer Rouge have captured worldwide attention in the years since their rise and fall, most notably through the 1984 movie *The Killing Fields*. The film portrays the horrors described in journalist Sydney Schanberg's book *The Death and Life of Dith Pran*.

# 11.   The Fall of Phnom Penh

P111 remained in the harbor, undergoing repairs for about a month before returning to duty. During that time, I found myself residing within the confines of an American training center. My temporary home was located strategically at the Navy Base, where rigorous military activities and drills were part of the daily routine.

In an abrupt turn of events that felt sudden and jarring, the American soldiers on the Cambodian base received orders to evacuate immediately. A fleet of helicopters cut through the serene morning sky, descending on our base with an air of finality. I prodded my superiors for information on what was happening, but all they would tell me was that I needed to go back home now.

The loud thunder of propellers filled the air—roars that echoed an unspoken precipitous danger. The Americans boarded the awaiting airships with grim faces. The whirling blades lifted them skyward and out to sea until our base was left uninhabited and vacant of any foreign presence.

Within minutes, all the captains from the Royal Cambodian Navy came together for an emergency meeting, and the base was filled with alarm. Captain Chrisna emerged from the conference with an unsettling look on his face. It was clear that worry had clawed its way into his grizzled mind.

"Sargent Ngin," he began, "we're in trouble. Phnom Penh has fallen to the Khmer Rouge."

His tone was grave and filled with panic.

"We must safeguard our families now," the captain told me. His voice emphasized the immediacy of his words. "Get your family together and get them aboard the ship at once!" he ordered.

"Where will we take them?" I asked, my eyes locked onto his.

"We'll take them to Phu Quoc Island, but we must get there swiftly."

His voice resonated with a mixture of fear and urgency.

Without wasting any time, I rushed directly to our living quarters. Inside, my father had already arrived before me. He sat gravely in the gloom-filled room, his face etched with worry. He was frantically informing my mother about the rapidly deteriorating conditions of Cambodia. My siblings—my brother and sisters hung on his every word absorbedly as he broke down details about our country's alarming collapse.

A sense of urgency gripped me as I turned toward my wife.

"We need to evacuate," I told her sternly yet reassuringly. My message was straightforward—we needed to board the departing ship without delay or risk being left behind amidst growing chaos.

My wife was eight months pregnant with our first child, a reason for joy and trepidation. Anxiety gnawed at me as I worried about the safety of my family in these uncertain times. Weighing the dangers, however, staying behind seemed far more hazardous than fleeing. The perils we faced at home overshadowed anything we could potentially face at sea.

In anticipation of the challenges ahead, I instructed my wife and mother to fill several pots with fresh water, ensuring we would have water to sustain us during our escape aboard the ship.

My brother, Sophon, stopped me as we prepared to leave the compound.

"I'm not going," he told me with a surprising certainty in his voice. I looked at him incredulously.

"What do you mean, 'You're not going?' You must go," I told him. "You have to come with us."

His face hardened into an expression of fierce determination that betrayed no trace of fear.

"No, Sophal, I have decided to stay back," he explained. "I'm going to protect the bay. That's my job."

His words hit me like a punch in the stomach.

"If you stay, you'll be killed," I warned him.

"You get our family to safety. Get Mom and Dad and our sisters out of here. Don't worry about me."

I might have been blind to the seriousness of our situation, but I thought that perhaps my brother would be alright. After all, these weren't foreign invaders we were facing. The Khmer Rouge were Cambodians, just like us. I couldn't imagine that they wanted to kill their fellow countrymen. I left my brother standing at the door of our home.

Crowds of people had gathered at the harbor where the ships lay anchored. Emotions ran high as a mixture of tearful faces stood alongside those screaming in fear and anticipation. In contrast, other individuals found some strange delight in the scenario, and their laughter carried across the docked vessels. One enthusiastic young man wanted to board the ship with his bicycle. Another had no intention of leaving his precious motorcycle behind, wheeling it through the crowd toward the ship's ramp. Yet, amid all this excitement lurked a palpable problem.

On the crowded deck of the ship, amidst a sea of passengers, one woman laboriously dragged a mattress on board. She flopped the mattress on the deck with determined steps and gestured for her children, husband, and other relatives to join her. They all dropped down on the mattress, creating their little oasis amid the chaos. They remained secluded on their private mattress island with a vast ocean of strangers surrounding them for the entire journey.

My family, along with the families of the other sailors, were safely aboard the ships. Other families living nearby heard of our departure and came to join us. News of the collapse had not yet reached the people living in the countryside, and many of them were left behind. Around two hundred fifty people boarded P111, a ship designed for twenty-eight sailors. P112 and P113 were likewise overflowing with similar numbers of hopeful escapees.

Every corner of the ships' decks was occupied. The beastly battleships that bobbed gently under the Cambodian sun were congested with people anxious to board with their myriad belongings. There appeared to be no room left on the decks of any of the three vessels.

The three battleships set out to sea.

The initial plan was to transport our families and loved ones to safety on Phu Quoc Island, then return with the ships to defend the bay. This plan was jeopardized as unrest teetered on full-blown chaos across our squadron of vessels. On each of the ships, a mounting disbelief began to spread. Several passengers started doubting the severity of the danger we faced. Their skepticism bred discontent, multiplying tensions on board. Other passengers wanted to return to the mainland to gather more of their family— children, parents, wives—and bring them to safety. This discord consequently led to verbal battles and physical confrontations aboard all three ships.

In the middle of the Bay of Thailand, amid the watery expanse surrounding us, the three captains commanded their ships to line up alongside each other. Captain Chrisna stood on the bridge of his commanding vessel with a grim expression. He understood the magnitude of his predicament; he could not return to the mainland. There was an undeniable finality in this realization.

"I'm a high-ranking officer," he told the other two captains. "I know if I go back, the Khmer Rouge will kill me. I'm guessing they'll do the same to you. If you want to head back to the mainland, then go, but I will not join you. It's your call."

After weighing our options and considering the insistence of those wishing to return, we decided to send one of the vessels, P113, back to the mainland with anyone who wanted to return home.

To facilitate movement across the watercraft, gangplanks were put into position, bridging each ship. This created easy access between all three ships as preparations were made for P113's imminent departure.

"When you reach the mainland," Captain Chrisna told the captain of P113, "radio back your situation. If things are good, we'll return and help you defend the bay."

Of the approximately seven hundred people on board the three vessels, two hundred were determined to go back. They boarded the departing battleship.

Captain Chrisna awaited word from the captain of P113. Time ticked by slowly. An hour turned into two hours—it had been enough time for the boat to complete its journey to the mainland. However, the radio remained silent. No transmission came through from the captain of P113, leaving us in suspended dread.

Captain Chrisna attempted to contact the captain of P113.

"P113, do you read me?" Captain Chrisna's voice crackled over the sound of the old French engines.

No response.

"Come in, P113. Do you read me?" Captain Chrisna repeated.

The speakers on board his ship crackled to life abruptly.

"This is P113," a voice responded. "Go ahead."

"This is Captain Chrisna of P111. I need to speak with the captain of P113."

"P111, return to base immediately," a gruff voice ordered. The authoritative urgency in the command was undisguised, almost tangible, but caught within the rhythm of static radio interference lurked a sinister back note— an unmistakable sound that chilled Captain Chrisna's spine—the bursting rattle of gunfire from automatic weapons.

"Yessir," responded Captain Chrisna. "May I speak with the captain of P113 first, sir?"

"That's not possible, Captain Chrisna," insisted the voice on the radio. "I am ordering you to return to base immediately." With the issuing of the deadly command, the catastrophic eruption of gunfire continued— an ominous symphony playing out across the radio waves of the two ships. The once serene air became punctuated by the sharp, vicious staccato of bullets flying—the frightening music to a macabre soundtrack that unraveled through the ship's speakers as pure torment and despair.

"Sir, I must speak with the captain."

"You must do one thing and one thing only, Captain Chrisna; you must return to base immediately. Am I making myself clear, Captain?"

Heart-wrenching cries for mercy echoed off the cold steel walls of P113, hauntingly pulsating over staticky radio waves.

The captain listened to the frantic pleas and piercing cries that bellowed above the blast of gunfire. The desperate appeals of the people on board P113 were nothing more than fading echoes highlighting their impending doom. All two hundred people aboard P113 were being slaughtered.

The Khmer Rouge had turned the vessel into a floating tomb for its terror-stricken sailors and innocent citizens.

"Let the crew know we cannot go back, Sergeant Ngin," Captain Chrisna told me. "If we do, we will all be killed."

## 12.    Open Waters

The Bay of Thailand stretched before me like a vast, empty void. The sky was a desolate expanse of blue, and the dark and lifeless water reflected the hollowness inside me. The rhythmic ebb and flow of the waves only intensified the sense of isolation and despair that engulfed me. I had lost everything that mattered: my friends, family, and home. The fate of my beloved brother, Sophon, consumed my thoughts, and the shadow of his loss kept me company like a constant companion on my lonely journey. Even my voice felt hollow and distant as if I were speaking into an abyss that could never be filled. The uncertainty of our situation and the absence of help or support made me feel more alone than ever. As we drifted aimlessly in the heart of the lonely bay,

I couldn't help but wonder if we would ever find refuge.

Given the current uncertainty, it would be unreasonable to proceed towards the island. Our new objective was to locate a secure harbor for docking. Each rolling wave on the silent, shifting sea symbolized another facet of our unforeseen devastation. Life for everyone aboard P111 and P112 had just taken a dramatic and devastating turn. In desperation, Captain Chrisna turned his vessel toward Thailand.

We had escaped the jaws of certain death, but the shadow of tragedy kept a relentless hold on us, tracing our course as if tethered by some unseen chain. Death may have been behind us, but misfortune took its place in stalking us. Before reaching the shores of Thailand, our ships ran out of fuel. P111 and P112 were adrift in the heart of the lonely bay.

By radio, Captain Chrisna contacted the port authorities of Thailand and Malaysia regarding our perilous plight. Sometime after that, a small patrol boat approached us. Two officials from the Port Authority of Thailand boarded P111. They spoke to our translator, and I could only watch the conversation unfold. Even if I could have heard them, I didn't speak Thai and wouldn't have understood their message. After a brief but seemingly heated discussion, the officials re-boarded their boat and returned to Thailand.

Our translator was tight-lipped about the conversation with the Thai officials. He only informed us that the Thai Government would not offer us any assistance. I was feeling uncertain and confused about the situation. Despite my efforts to seek clarification, the translator remained silent about his discussions with the Thai authorities. Our translator's lack of transparency added to our mounting frustration. The absence of assistance from the Thai Government forced us to reassess our plans and find alternative solutions.

Despite being sympathetic to our plight, the Government of Malaysia was still determining what help they could extend. They offered refuge to the Muslim passengers on board, and approximately six individuals chose to disembark and stay in Malaysia. However, Malaysian authorities could not provide sanctuary for the remaining group, so they suggested we continue our journey towards Indonesia or Singapore for further assistance. Despite the setback, their guidance pointed us towards potential solutions and alternative destinations that could offer aid and support in our time of need.

The Malaysian people were unaware of Phnom Penh's overthrow. News of this city's fall had reached only Cambodia, Vietnam, and Laos by then. Nonetheless, their empathy was evident in their generous actions towards us. The Malaysian Government generously dispatched a substantial amount of food, clothing, medicine, and fuel to us. We received their crucial aid with immense gratitude, as it significantly alleviated some of our hardships.

Dealing with uncertainty and feeling stranded at sea affected our morale. The prospect of finding refuge in the Philippines brought a glimmer of hope amidst the challenges we faced. The Malaysian Government sent two ships to escort us toward Indonesia, but after about twenty miles, they turned back.

The people of Indonesia were also unaware of Cambodia's collapse until they spotted us on our two ships searching for safety. Our women were allowed to disembark in Indonesia to shower, but the men were forced to stay on board the vessel. The People of Indonesia sailed out to our ships with supplies of food and fruit. This was the first time I had ever seen an orange. I was utterly captivated by the sight of this bright-colored fruit. The fruit in Cambodia had always been green; here was this vibrantly colored orange. This marked my inaugural encounter with the vivid, radiant hue and succulent juiciness of an orange, an entirely novel experience for me.

A day or two later, the American Ambassador visited our ship. We talked with him about our situation and sought guidance on where to turn for help next. Unfortunately, despite our hopes, Indonesia was not an option for us. The Ambassador regretfully shared that he could not provide us shelter in Indonesia or Singapore. However, he could offer assistance if we sailed to the Philippines.

The Ambassador's visit left us with mixed emotions—gratitude for his willingness to offer aid and frustration at our limited choices. Nevertheless, we were determined to persevere and explore all possible avenues toward securing safety. We steered our ships from Singapore toward the Philippines with no other course of action.

The ships struggled to maintain their speed as they were weighed down by the sheer number of passengers onboard. The open waters stretched before them, but their excessive load hindered their progress. The engines strained to propel the vessels forward, causing them to move sluggishly, only about fifteen to twenty knots. The decks were crowded with people, jostling for space and struggling to find a comfortable spot. The crew members of P111 were given priority in choosing their locations. I directed my family to settle near the ship's smokestack for some added warmth during the chilly nights at sea. The cool sea breeze and the sound of waves crashing against the hull created a serene atmosphere amid the tragedy of war.

My parents, two sisters, pregnant wife, and I huddled beside the smokestack. As night fell, the ship's lights illuminated the stark scene. We watched as stars began to twinkle above us. Amidst this chaos, my family's chosen spot near the smokestack became a sanctuary, offering physical warmth and emotional comfort as we journeyed across the open sea.

My wife, with a swollen belly beneath her trembling hands, looked at me with fear in her eyes as chaos engulfed us. The air was thick with the sounds of children's cries blending with the moans of adults who were ill and scared. A sense of helplessness and uncertainty surrounded us. I felt a surge of protectiveness for my wife and our unborn child, wanting nothing more than to shield them from the turmoil surrounding us. The rigidity in her grip on her belly spoke volumes about her anxiety and concern for our baby's safety.

As I scanned the surrounding faces, I saw expressions of confusion and desperation. The weight of the situation hung heavily in the air, making it hard to breathe amid the discord of desperation. Despite the crowdedness on board, we felt isolated then, separated from the rest of the world by the vast and terrifying South China Sea. My heart clenched at the sight of so many suffering individuals, each fighting their personal battles against anguish and uncertainty. But at that moment, all I could do was hold onto my wife tightly, offering her whatever comfort and reassurance I could muster.

After days at sea, the translator who had spoken with the port authorities from Thailand opened up about what had transpired with the Thai Port Authority. He told us that the Thai Government had not approached us with plans to extend their assistance. They weren't there to provide help or protection as we had expected. Thailand's intervention was far from humanitarian. Instead, their interest lay in alarming motives, and their actions were steered by predatory greed rather than kindness. The Thai Government was interested in purchasing the women on board our vessel.

This shocking revelation left us all in a state of disbelief and anger. Instead of offering aid to helpless, homeless, and nationless women who had been subjected to the unimaginable horrors of war, the Thai Government was trying to exploit them for human trafficking. The audacity of the proposal itself shattered my faith in humanity.

"'These are not commodities,' I told them," the translator said. "'These are human beings with rights and dignity.'"

"Why didn't you tell us sooner?" I asked him.

"I knew how angry it would make you. I was afraid of how you would react."

This unexpected proposal from the Thai Government was a stark reminder of the realities we contended with during this crisis.

On the third day of our journey, the endless expanse of the deep, dark ocean surrounded us as we sailed. While most passengers were fast asleep, I was wide awake in the dead of night. The slow but steady movement of the ship was only interrupted by the rhythmic sound of someone snoring, the occasional cough, or the cries of a hungry child.

I sat on the deck, admiring the twinkling stars above and feeling the cool breeze against my skin. Gazing out into the vastness of the sea, I couldn't help but feel a mix of awe and unease at being surrounded by such immense and mysterious waters. A full moon cast an eerie glow over the water, creating a sense of tranquility that was hauntingly beautiful.

I leaned over to my wife, excitement in my voice.

"Honey, do you see the moon?" I asked her, filled with wonder at its beauty. "Look how big and beautiful and bright it is!"

Peering up at the sky, she responded, "Where? Where is it, Sophal?"

"Look up," I urged her, pointing towards the bright, beautiful moon overhead. "Look up at the sky."

"I don't see any moon," she told me.

"C'mon," I encouraged her, puzzled by her response, "Don't lie!"

"I'm not lying, Sophal. I see your hand pointing upwards, but I don't see the moon."

I was terrified when I realized that my wife was experiencing pregnancy blindness. In the Cambodian culture, it's believed that some pregnant women lose their ability to see clearly, especially for far-off distances. Instead, they can only focus on things up close. Psychologists sometimes refer to this condition as hysterical blindness. When I realized the implications, a wave of concern for my wife's well-being washed over me. I gently took her head in my hands and held her close to my chest, feeling the tears welling up in my eyes.

"I'm sorry, husband," she told me. "I didn't see it. I didn't see the moon."

Her vulnerability in that moment struck me deeply. I couldn't shake off the fear that she may never see again. The weight of the situation bore heavily on my shoulders as I tried to provide comfort amidst this new concern.

I whispered words of reassurance into her ear, hoping to convey some sense of comfort despite the overwhelming uncertainty. It was distressing to see her struggle with such a debilitating symptom. Overcome by emotion, I broke down.

"Why are you crying, Sophal?" she asked gently.

"Because you're not well," I said. "You're not strong, and you don't have medicine to support the baby; you don't have food to eat."

I couldn't bear seeing her weak and without support for our soon-to-arrive baby. I felt helpless, knowing we didn't have enough medicine or food.

"It's okay, husband. It will be okay. Tell me, how long until we reach the Philippines?"

"I don't know," I told her. "Maybe another three more weeks. Maybe more."

She gently guided my hand to her abdomen, positioning it on top of our child.

"Do you feel that, Sophal?" she inquired softly.

A fluttering sensation beneath my palm surprised me as I placed my hand on her stomach.

"That's the baby kicking," she explained with a tender smile.

The pulsing movements of the unborn child seemed almost magical as I felt them for the first time. A sense of wonder washed over me, realizing that new life was growing inside her. I marveled at this tiny being developing and moving within her womb. It was a fleeting yet profound moment that would stay etched in my memory forever—a glimpse into the precious journey of parenthood unfolding in an ocean of fear and trepidation.

Days passed, and the once clear sky became obscured by ominous clouds, casting a dark, foreboding shadow over the turbulent sea below. The water grew dark and black. Storm clouds loomed on the horizon. We watched as the darkening clouds moved toward us. The powerful storm struck with little warning, releasing a deluge of rain upon our ship. The vessel rocked violently in the turbulent waves. Lightning cracked across the sky as thunder boomed overhead, adding to the sense of danger and urgency. Despite efforts to maintain stability, the ship struggled against the relentless onslaught of wind and waves.

The once calm atmosphere turned chaotic, with cries and screams ringing out across the deck. Some sought solace in prayer, calling on God for protection and safety. Each lurch of the ship brought renewed terror to those onboard, amplifying their pleas for divine intervention.

Despite the terror of the storm, we needed the water. With every ounce of determination, we banded together, stripping off articles of clothing and fashioning them into makeshift funnels. We knotted shirts to skirts, tied pants together, and nearly anything that could hold water was utilized in this desperate quest. Buckets, pots, and any available receptacle were swiftly filled with the precious liquid.

We found ourselves in a dire situation as we not only faced a shortage of food and water but also grappled with the mounting fear of disease spreading among us on the ship. The cramped living conditions and lack of proper sanitation facilities made it too easy for illness to take hold. With limited medical supplies and no access to professional healthcare, our anxiety grew even more palpable. As the days dragged on, each cough or sniffle prompted heightened concern that it could spiral into a full-blown outbreak. We took every precaution we could think of. However, the constant unease lingered over us like an ominous cloud.

Captain Chrisna patrolled the deck in his white uniform daily. One morning, he noticed a distressed mother with a tiny baby who wasn't moving.

"If your baby dies," Captain Chrisna told the young mother, "You will have to throw it into the ocean, or it will spread disease."

"Please, let me keep my baby," the mother pleaded with the captain, looking directly into his eyes. "Let me bury her when we are on land."

Women in Cambodia are traditionally expected to be modest and soft-spoken. They are to be well-mannered and refined. Traditionally, they are to be "light walkers"— so quiet in their movements that you cannot hear their silk skirts rustling. This woman's confrontation with a male military commander was unheard of and considered highly inappropriate. A woman would never have even looked into the face of such a man as Captain Chrisna, let alone speaking so directly to him.

The captain turned away from the distressed mother without another word.

The little girl lay in her mother's arms, her tiny body weak from days without food. Her mother had gathered just enough water to sustain her, drawing tiny sips to her parched lips. Even as hunger gnawed at her belly and exhaustion weighed heavy on her limbs, the child clung to life. Driven by her mother's unwavering hope and an indomitable spirit, the baby girl clung to life.

Time seemed to stand still during our relentless voyage across the vast, endless ocean. The sun beat down on us mercilessly, casting a golden hue over the shimmering water. The waves rose and fell hypnotically, lulling us into a trance-like state. Our ship creaked and groaned with each movement as if protesting the ceaseless journey.

Each day blurred into the next as routine tasks became our only anchor to reality. The distant horizon taunted us with its elusive promise of land beyond reach. But still, we pressed on with unwavering determination, fueled by the hope of reaching the Philippine Islands.

Nights were spent under a canopy of glittering stars, offering a brief respite from the unforgiving daylight hours. Yet, despite our challenges and hardships, there was a certain beauty in this relentless voyage—a sense of freedom and adventure that could not be replicated anywhere else.

Over time, the relentless embrace of the sea left my skin encrusted with a salty film, a reminder of the endless expanse around me. My once-trimmed hair had grown unruly, flowing and dancing in the ocean breeze. The length of my beard had increased and was now hanging down nearly to my belly.

I was filled with wonder as I laid eyes on dolphins for the first time. Their smooth bodies moved effortlessly through the water, a display of grace and precision that left me in awe, creating a harmonious dance between sea and sky. As I watched, another unexpected sight came: flying fish soaring out of the water like glittering projectiles. Each leap illuminated the air with a dazzling spectacle, making me gasp in wonder at nature's beauty. It was a breathtaking experience that etched itself into my memory forever.

As we sailed towards the Philippines, our anticipation was tinged with a touch of unease. The vast expanse of the ocean held daunting secrets. One day, as the sun cast its golden hue upon the water, I spotted sleek shapes cutting through the waves. At first glance, they seemed like sinuous ribbons dancing in harmony with the currents. As my gaze sharpened, a dreadful fear gripped me. The sinewy forms were not harmless ribbons but slithering serpents, their scales glistening malevolently under the sunlight. The sight sent a ripple of fear through me, and tales of sea serpents and their deadly venom flooded my mind.

In addition to the menacing snakes, we also caught sight of majestic whales breaching nearby. However, our initial awe quickly turned to anxiety as we worried about being mistaken for prey by these colossal creatures. The thought of being swallowed whole by a creature of such immense size made me tremble. I grew anxious that any moment could bring too close an encounter with one of these formidable marine predators.

My family occupied the same cramped space next to the smokestack for an entire month. We spent our days huddled together, finding ways to pass the time and maintain our sanity amidst the oppressive conditions. Each day seemed to blur into the next as we struggled to find moments of respite and relief from our relentless discomfort. One passenger described it as being "squeezed together like a row of grilled catfish on a stick."

After almost thirty days at sea, our spirits were lifted as we spotted a search plane in the distance. The sight of the aircraft brought a glimmer of hope, igniting a surge of excitement among the crew and passengers. After enduring weeks of isolation and uncertainty, the possibility of rescue was tangible. The once desolate horizon now held our potential salvation, and we clung to that hope with all our might.

# 13. Ocean Waves to Shock Waves

After spending nearly a month at sea, battling unpredictable weather and dwindling supplies, the sight of the search plane flying overhead brought us relief. Our spirits lifted as hope washed over us, knowing that help was finally near. We had been alone at sea for seemingly an eternity, and the plane's engines above us filled us with renewed hope. The sight of the aircraft reassured us that our ordeal was finally coming to an end.

Captain Chrisna established a radio connection with the search plane. The crackling of static faded as the voices of our rescuers came through loud and clear. With a tone of urgency but calm authority, Captain

Chrisna relayed critical information about the status of his crew and passengers. The U.S. Navy search plane acknowledged the update with a swift response, affirming that they were ready to assist in any way possible.

Before granting us passage into the bay, we were commanded to cast all our personal belongings into the ocean. Those who had brought backpacks, bicycles, motorcycles, and even mattresses were ordered to throw them off the vessel and watch as they disappeared beneath the rippling waves and into the depths below.

When our ship docked at the American Naval Base in the Philippines in the early evening, officers directed us to disembark in groups. We were required to exit as families. I left the ship with my parents, wife, and two sisters. Upon arrival, the men and women were separated and led to distinct areas to shower.

As I entered the showers, a wave of steam hit me as warm water cascaded down from above. The sweet smell of soap filled the air. I lathered up and rinsed off, shedding layers of dirt, salt, and exhaustion. The feeling of cleanliness was so refreshing that I breathed a sigh of relief as I scrubbed away the grime and salt from my body. The hot water felt like a luxury I had almost forgotten existed. Slowly, I began to feel human again, invigorated by this simple act of bathing.

After finishing our showers, clean towels were provided for us to dry off with. We wrapped ourselves in the soft cloth, feeling a sense of comfort and normalcy return to us. It was a small gesture that meant so much after everything we had been through. The showers had washed away not just the physical grime but also some of the weariness in our souls.

We were then provided with fresh sets of clothes to change into. The soft fabric was a welcome change from the worn-out garments we had been wearing for weeks. Once dressed, we were led to a bustling mess hall and given warm meals.

We ate well for the first time in a month and were directed to individual tents arranged on the base. Each tent in this refugee camp was equipped with beds and basic amenities for our comfort. As we settled into our tents, family by family, the surroundings gradually quieted as night fell. The peace and tranquility of the evening enveloped us, providing a welcomed break from our harrowing journey.

A cool breeze gently brushed against the tent flaps, inducing a sense of relaxation. Stars twinkled in the dark sky above, illuminating our temporary home. Amidst this peaceful setting, we drifted off to sleep, grateful for the shelter and safety provided by our temporary abode on the base.

On the second full day of our stay at the base, my wife went into labor. The soldiers acted swiftly and rushed her to a hospital in the nearby city for medical attention. I was not allowed to accompany her. Three long days passed before my wife returned to the refugee camp, holding our newborn baby girl in her arms. Holding my daughter for the first time brought tears to my eyes, a precious moment amidst the chaos of our situation.

The child was so small. Her fragile, diminutive frame made her look like a little monkey. Strangely, she never cried. The American doctors and nurses on the base were accommodating and supportive.

During our time in the Philippines, we attended educational classes focused on familiarizing us with various aspects of the United States. Our instructors emphasized vital elements such as language, lifestyle, and cultural diversity within American society. It was as if a cultural shock wave had hit me. A defining moment came when we were introduced to the concept that Americans are often categorized based on three primary skin colors: white, black, and red. This notion of 'red' people, a term we had never encountered before, sparked our curiosity and confusion, adding a layer of intrigue to our cultural exploration.

"What do you mean by red?" I asked my teacher.

"Those are the Indians," they told us. "They are the native Americans."

As Cambodians, we were called 'gold' or yellow-skinned people. We later learned that this terminology is rooted in centuries-old ideologies and perceptions about race and ethnicity. The association of Cambodians with gold or yellow skin reflects broader attitudes towards Southeast Asian populations and their physical features, a legacy of historical interactions and cultural exchanges.

Regarding language, the most English I could speak was "What is your name?" and "My name is Sophal." The Cambodian alphabet, known as Khmer script, significantly differs from the Latin alphabet used in

America. It consists of 33 consonants and 23 vowels, with each letter representing a unique sound. The script is written from left to right, similar to English. Despite the differences, many Cambodians are familiar with the Latin alphabet due to the influence of French colonization in Cambodia during the 19th and 20th centuries.

While studying the English language, I discovered that many words in English had origins rooted in French when the Normans brought their language and culture across the English Channel in 1066. As a result, English absorbed a plethora of French vocabulary, particularly in areas such as law, art, cuisine, and fashion. Words like restaurant, ballet, chic, and entrepreneur have seamlessly integrated into the English lexicon, simplifying some of my learning.

I had a difficult time pronouncing the word 'water.' Americans pronounce the word like 'WAD-der,' but I pronounced it 'wah-TER.' This was one of the many linguistic hurdles I faced while learning English. Another difference between the Cambodian and English languages is the use of personal pronouns. Americans use personal pronouns instead of noun phrases to refer to people and things already identified. The words, he, she, it, they, them, have no equivalent in the Khmer script. If someone asks, 'Where's the spoon?' And you answer, 'It's in the drawer.' Cambodians would not understand what you mean by the word 'it.' If I came to your house and asked you, 'Is your brother home?' and you told me, 'He's not home right now.' I wouldn't understand what 'he' meant. Khmer script has no equivalent for the word 'he.' In Cambodian, we would say, 'My brother is not home,' or, 'The spoon is in the drawer.'

We stayed in the Philippines, taking classes and adjusting to cultural changes, for about a week. At that time, the United States had established three refugee camps to accommodate those seeking shelter. Located in California, Texas, and Pennsylvania, these camps served as our temporary homes until we could find sponsors. Unfortunately, the California and Texas camps had reached total capacity by then. Consequently, my family boarded a plane headed to the camp in Pennsylvania. My wife, our newborn baby, and I were assigned three seats on an airplane. We were not allowed to hold our tiny baby on our laps. She had to be in her own seat. This was the first time we had heard our baby cry.

The moment our baby's cries filled the air, it was as if hope had suddenly blossomed within us. Usually, a crying baby on an airplane is an annoyance, but her cries were joyful to us. The other families, seated together in this journey towards an uncertain future, erupted into cheers and applause.

"Hey, Sophal," they called out, their voices filled with genuine happiness, "your baby woke up! She's alive."

Tears of gratitude welled in our eyes as we gazed at our precious newborn daughter, realizing the magnitude of this small but monumental victory amidst our shared struggle for survival. Her cries became a beacon of hope and joy in that fleeting moment, surrounded by uncertainty.

Once we had settled in Pennsylvania, we were asked for all kinds of information.

Did you go to high school?

Did you go to college?

What type of work do you do?

Do you still have family members in Cambodia?

I told them about my aunt, uncle, and cousins, and especially about my brother, Sophon, who had remained behind after we sailed out of the Bay of Kompong Son. They documented everything.

They also required that every man in the camp attend English classes and learn to read and write in English.

Eventually, my family was sponsored by a Virginian Bishop from the Episcopalian Church. Since we were still learning about the American lifestyle and culture, we were instructed not to do anything without our sponsor's permission or consent.

My family and I were instructed to board a bus bound for Virginia and meet our sponsor upon arrival. This was a daunting task for me. I had seemingly endless questions running through my mind now. How would I know when and where to get off the bus? How would I recognize my sponsor? What if no one showed up to meet us at the bus station?

The thought of navigating to an unfamiliar destination without knowing where to disembark or who awaited us filled me with uncertainty and anxiety. The idea of venturing into an unknown place without guidance or assurance left me feeling apprehensive and ill-prepared. The language barrier added another layer of complexity to the already challenging situation.

I was reassured that this was a bus specifically designated to transport refugees and that the driver would know where to take me and where to let me off. We were also given name tags so anyone who saw us could recognize that we were refugees.

The bus trip to Richmond, Virginia, seemed almost as unnerving as the boat trip to the Philippine Islands. After arriving at the Richmond bus station, I noticed Robert Bachman holding a sign written in the Khmer script that read, 'Ngin Family.' Robert was the pastor of a local Christian church.

My wife and I approached him with our baby girl, and he shouted a warm and friendly greeting.

"Hi! How are you?"

We bowed to him, lowering our heads respectfully, but he reached out, grabbed our hands, and shook them enthusiastically. It's hard to imagine the surprise on our faces at this gesture.

In Cambodia, traditional greetings involve a gesture called a *sampeah*. This gesture consists in placing both palms together in front of the chest, resembling a lotus flower. The level at which the hands are placed varies depending on the recipient of the greeting.

For peers, the *sampeah* is carried out at chest height, while for elders or higher-ranking individuals, it is done at mouth level. When greeting parents, grandparents, or teachers, the hands are raised to nose level. Kings and monks receive a *sampeah* at eyebrow level as a sign of utmost respect.

Lastly, hands are raised to forehead level during prayer or when greeting deities. This traditional greeting is deeply ingrained in Cambodian culture and expresses reverence and respect for others.

"Don't worry. Look up," he told us. "Look at me."

We simply continued to bow.

At that time, the United States Government paid $300.00 a month to each refugee, which our sponsor used to pay our living expenses. With the $900.00 I received, $300.00 each for myself, my wife, and our baby, our sponsor found us an apartment in Richmond. He enrolled me in day classes,

where I studied English as a second language. At night, from about six o'clock until midnight, I worked in a grocery store as a janitor for two dollars an hour.

Our sponsor also filled out several forms asking us about family we had left behind in Cambodia. We gave him the name of my brother, Sophon, along with the names of aunts, uncles, and cousins we had left behind. These forms were sent to the Office of Immigration in Washington, D.C.

We encountered a lot of hatred and racism in Virginia. People seem to be angry with the refugees. They would swear at us and call us names. They'd push us out of their way if we walked too slowly along the sidewalk.

They would tell me that the government took their tax money to bring me over from Cambodia and to support me over here. They insisted I was taking jobs away from American citizens. They also accused me of not paying taxes and refused to listen when I tried to show them I paid taxes just like they did.

This all was so unsettling to me. I thought that if Henry Kissinger hadn't illegally bombed Cambodia, the Cambodian government wouldn't have collapsed. I would still be living in my hometown, serving in the Cambodian Navy. Because of *Operation Menu* and the illegal activities under the Nixon regime, my life was placed in jeopardy by the American government. I didn't come to America to take jobs from other people. I came to America because if I had stayed in Cambodia, I would have been murdered by the communist regime. These unsettling experiences in Virginia may have made my next life-altering decision easier, but they also empowered me to take control of my future.

After one year of living and working in Richmond, VA, I received a message from a Cambodian man I had met in the Pennsylvania refugee camp. A family in Utah had sponsored him. He suggested I move there for better job opportunities and more manageable living conditions. He said Utah had plenty of work opportunities and was more conducive to making a living. He mentioned that he had personally been working at a mushroom farm in Filmore for the past year.

Finding a better job in Virginia proved difficult, and I struggled to make a living as a grocery store janitor. The idea of relocating to Utah seemed appealing, especially considering the positive feedback he provided about the job market there. Hearing about his experiences working at the mushroom farm piqued my curiosity. I started contemplating the possibility of moving and exploring what Utah had to offer.

The thought of beginning a new chapter in my life in Utah excited me. It felt like an opportunity for growth and advancement that I couldn't overlook. This unexpected message opened possibilities I hadn't previously considered, sparking a sense of adventure and exploration.

I had purchased my first car for $1000. It was a used AMC Gremlin, one of history's dorkiest automobiles. Few vehicles have more reprehensible roots than the AMC Gremlin. Named for the mythical creatures said to be responsible for crashing airplanes and breaking machinery, it was introduced to the public on April Fool's Day. And as for the styling, AMC

design chief Dick Teague made his first sketch of the car on the back of a Northwest Orient Airlines barf bag.

Yet, for all that, the Gremlin was arguably AMC's most innovative car: It was inexpensive to develop, and its timing was flawless. I determined to pack up the Gremlin and head out West, a decision that required courage and resilience.

A week before we set out on our new adventure, I told my sponsor that we were moving.

"Where are you moving to? Where will you go?" he asked me with concern and surprise.

"We are moving to Utah," I told him.

"Utah?" he said with increased concern and surprise. "Don't move to Utah. They're all bad people out there. Don't go there. They'll take all your money."

Regardless of our sponsor's warning, we embarked on our journey to the West with a U-Haul trailer packed full of our belongings and the Gremlin loaded to the hilt. My two sisters had married Cambodian gentlemen in the refugee camp, and they decided to join us on this adventure to Utah. The decision to move out West was filled with excitement and anticipation for new beginnings.

As we hit the road, the landscape changed from Virginia's familiar surroundings to vast open spaces stretching before us. The thought of starting fresh in a new place brought mixed emotions but mostly a sense of hope and excitement for the opportunities ahead in Utah.

The journey was not just a physical one but also an emotional transition as we embraced the unknown future waiting for us out West. Each mile brought us closer to our destination, building anticipation for the adventures awaiting us in Utah.

We forged ahead into another vast unknown, united by family ties and the shared dream of a better tomorrow in yet another new location.

# 14. Mushrooms and Mormons

We had planned to drive straight from Virginia to Utah, but a massive snowstorm that closed the highway for two days delayed us in Colorado Springs.

Upon arriving in Fillmore, we settled into a cozy residence situated within the mushroom farm. The gray and blue building on the west side of I-15 didn't look like much. The business was Mountain View Mushrooms. They had only been in operation since 1974.

The business does everything from composting material, spawning and seeding hundreds of wooden trays, and harvesting, packing, and shipping mushrooms. Most don't recognize the company's name because its customers are mainly restaurants. People don't see them in grocery stores.

Our supervisor welcomed us warmly and familiarized us with our fellow workers. The farm, with its innovative approach of constructing rentable homes on the property, fostered a strong sense of community among us. This unique living arrangement not only improved our living conditions but also strengthened our bond as we shared a common living environment.

The first year in Fillmore was particularly challenging for us, having grown up in the jungles of Cambodia. The heavy snowfall that blanketed the town was a stark contrast to the tropical climate we were used to. The thick layers of snow often made it difficult to navigate through the streets and significantly limited visibility. We struggled to adapt to the cold temperatures and found it hard to stay warm despite bundling up in layers of winter clothing.

In spite of our initial challenges, we persevered, slowly learning to cope with the extreme weather patterns that characterized winters in Fillmore. Over time, we began to appreciate the unique beauty of the winter landscape. Through determination and resilience, we gradually acclimated to our new surroundings, embracing the hardships and joys of living in a snowy town.

Fillmore itself was small, with only three trees scattered throughout its streets. Basic amenities were scarce. There was only one gas station, a small grocery store, and a breakfast and coffee shop. The courthouse stood as the prominent landmark in the area.

After a long day at the mushroom farm, the employees would gather by the river to fish for dinner. The serene riverside setting provided a peaceful escape from the demands of our job. Fishing provided food and connected us with nature and each other after a hard day's work on the farm.

Despite catching plenty of carp, we were hesitant to eat them after being told that carp was not a preferred fish in the area. Local residents preferred catching trout or whitefish, which were considered more desirable options.

Our supervisors treated us more like family than mere employees, which was very different from how we retreated in Virginia. The people in Utah were kind, and even though Utah has a vastly different climate than Cambodia and our traditions, religions, and language are so different, I still felt more at home here than anywhere else I had been since our escape from the Khmer regime.

Our supervisor was incredibly kind. I asked a Cambodian friend about his kindness and seemingly genuine concern for our well-being. He explained that his behavior stemmed from being a member of the Church of Jesus Christ of Latter-day Saints, where he held the position of Bishop. I had limited knowledge about Christian churches, so terms like Latter-day Saint and Bishop were unfamiliar. My friend explained that our supervisor's conduct toward us was driven by his religious beliefs and values. His role in his church was pivotal in shaping his approach toward how he treated others. I soon gained greater insight into the principles guiding my supervisor's conduct. I recognized how his religion played an integral part in influencing his actions.

One of the challenges we faced in Fillmore was the limited shopping and dining options. If we were craving a chicken dinner, we had to drive a little over a hundred miles to Provo to buy it. Provo was also home to a well-stocked grocery store called Reams, which was always a treat for us to visit.

Entering Reams would fill us with excitement as we explored the aisles of fresh produce and food supplies not readily available in Fillmore. Monthly trips to Provo became essential to stocking up on our pantry items. The journey back to Fillmore with bags full of groceries from Reams ensured we would have everything we needed. Access to a full-service grocery store in Provo bridged the gap between Fillmore's culinary limitations and our desire for variety and fresh produce.

While visiting Provo, I bumped into another Cambodian while shopping at Reams supermarket. He approached me after overhearing me speak Cambodian to my mother. He lived in Salt Lake City and recommended that I consider moving my family there, mentioning the availability of suitable apartments for rent. He assured me there were job opportunities when I expressed concern about finding work.

His offer sparked a glimmer of hope as I considered the possibility of starting fresh in Salt Lake City. The idea of relocating to a new city seemed daunting yet intriguing. It was time for a change, a new beginning for my family. With his encouragement, I entertained the thought of uprooting our lives and embarking on a new adventure in Salt Lake City.

# 15.  Joseph Smith Speaks Cambodian?

I secured a job with a company based in Sandy, Utah, that specialized in manufacturing parts for medical equipment, particularly EKG machines. I was hired to work in the assembly department. To ensure our children were taken care of, my wife and I coordinated our schedules—she worked the night shift while I worked during the day. This arrangement ensured that one of us was always home to look after our two young daughters. It was challenging, but we balanced work and family responsibilities effectively. Our focus was on creating a stable environment for our children and building a better future for our family.

In the small town of Sandy, there were only a handful of Cambodian families compared to Fillmore, where the community was more abundant. Despite our smaller numbers, we would all come together on paydays or special Cambodian holidays to celebrate and honor our heritage. These gatherings were special occasions for us to share memories and traditions.

I took great pride in cooking my favorite Cambodian dishes, savoring the flavors that reminded us of home. The aroma of lemongrass and turmeric filled the air as we prepared traditional meals like amok and bai sach chrouk. It was a way for us to pass down our culture to the younger generation and keep our customs alive. These gatherings were not just about food but also about preserving our identity and strengthening our sense of community.

Despite being far from Cambodia, these moments allowed us to maintain a piece of our cultural identity amid a different world. We found comfort and unity in each other's company through food and tradition. And as we sat down together to enjoy our meals, we felt connected to our past and hopeful for the future.

One sunny Saturday afternoon, I was home from work and decided to take a much-needed nap. As I drifted off, a knock at the door jolted me awake. Groggily, I reached the door and hesitantly opened it to find two young men in white shirts and ties standing there. They were American missionaries.

They greeted me as a brother and wanted to talk about God. I told them I already knew about God.

"That's great," they told me. "So, what religion are you?"

"I am Buddhist," I responded.

"Oh. So, where are you from?" they asked.

I told them I came from Cambodia, but I don't think they understood much about my country because they asked me if I was from Hawaii.

The majority of Southeast Asian countries—countries like China, Vietnam, Japan, and Thailand—all worship Buddha, but not the same Buddha. China, Japan, and Vietnam worship a heavy, fat Buddha, while Cambodia, Laos, and Thailand worship a thinner Buddha.

My parents would take me to the Buddhist temple in Phnom Penh. We would sit in front of a giant statue of Buddha, and we considered him a god. My grandma would bring food as a donation for the monks.

Feeling uncertain about engaging in a religious discussion, I told them I didn't understand what they were talking about and declined their offer by closing the door on them. As best as I can recall, my exact words were, "Good-bye. Be gone. Go away."

About three months later, a young man appeared at my doorstep unannounced. Before I could respond, he greeted me reverently in Cambodian, addressing me as 'Uncle Sophal.' In Cambodia, the term 'uncle' expresses respect for elders. He then offered me the traditional Cambodian greeting, the 'sampeah,' a gesture performed by placing the palms together in front of the body.

Surprised by this unexpected display of familiarity, this courteous gesture left me puzzled and intrigued. He then spoke to me in my native language, which shocked and delighted me. As he stood in the doorway, I couldn't help but wonder what had led him to seek me out.

"May I visit with you today in your house?" the Cambodian-speaking gentleman asked. The encounter stirred a particular curiosity within me to delve deeper into his background and intentions, so I welcomed him into my home and called my wife and children to meet him.

The new visitor told me his name was Artie Johnson. He was a missionary from the Church of Jesus Christ of Latter-day Saints. He had been serving in the Church's newest temple in Washington, D.C. He mentioned seeing my name on an ID-94 refugee form indicating that I had moved to Utah.

In Virginia, I had discovered a diverse array of Christian religions. Among them were Catholics and Protestants, each with their own distinct beliefs and traditions. Despite this rich tapestry of faiths, I must admit that my knowledge about these various denominations could have been improved. I didn't understand the differences between the Church of Jesus Christ of Latter-day Saints and other Christian religions.

We talked about what I do for a living: making medical devices. We spoke at length about my journey from Virginia to Utah. He was surprised to learn that we had driven across the country. I told him we had been stranded in Colorado Springs due to a heavy snowstorm, and we eventually arrived in Filmore. We talked about my decision to move to Sandy to get away from so much snow and have easier access to food and groceries.

He was delighted to learn about my family and seemed genuinely happy to meet us. He asked if he could come back and visit us again. I told him he could stop by on Saturdays if he came early in the afternoon.

Two or three weeks after his first visit, Artie Johnson returned once more with a special gift—a copy of the Book of Mormon. At the time of his visit, this sacred text had only been partially translated into Cambodian.

I asked him if it was a bible.

"It's not *the* Bible, but it is a volume of scripture, translated by Joseph Smith, a prophet of God."

I did not know the word 'prophet' then, so Artie Johnson looked it up in his English-Cambodian dictionary. He then told me that Joseph Smith was a ព្យាការី (pyeakeari.)

"Would you like to learn the story about Joseph Smith?" he asked me.

"Yes," I told him, "I'd like to hear about Joseph Smith."

We had lunch together. We discussed the prophet Joseph Smith, Nephi, and the Book of Mormon. Artie told me he wanted me to meet his family. He talked about the two years he had spent serving as a missionary in Cambodia. I didn't know the English word missionary at that time, so Artie Johnson showed me in his Cambodian dictionary what missionary អ្នកផ្សព្វផ្សាយសាសនា (anak phsaapvophsaeay sasanea) was in Cambodian.

"Uncle Sophal, maybe you don't understand a lot of English, but will you read this Cambodian translation of the Book of Mormon?" he asked me with a hopeful gleam in his eyes.

Surprised, I questioned him about why I should read it.

"Because," he explained, "this book contains God's word revealed to Joseph Smith by the Angel Moroni."

I had heard the term angel before, but I didn't fully grasp the meaning of the word. The missionary explained to me that the Book of Mormon had been given to Joseph Smith by

Moroni, an ទេវតា (tevta) of God, and that the prophet Joseph had translated the book from its original ancient text. My initial response was surprise—I mistakenly thought Joseph Smith had translated the Book of Mormon into Cambodian.

"So, Joseph Smith speaks Cambodian?" I asked.

"No. No, Uncle Sophal," Artie chuckled. He then clarified that Joseph Smith had translated the ancient text into English using sacred tools and divine guidance. The Church had made subsequent translations into other languages over the years. Artie Johnson left the copy of the Book of Mormon on our table.

"Tonight, you read this, okay?" he told me.

I agreed to read it. Despite Artie's kind gesture, the book remained untouched for two weeks until Artie returned and inquired about my progress.

"Did you read the Book of Mormon, Sophal?"

I confessed that I hadn't even opened it. Arty looked so disappointed.

"Uncle Sophal," he told me, "Read it! Please read it. If you have any concerns, it's okay, we can read it together. You read in Cambodian, and I'll follow along in English."

"Okay, Artie." I finally told him, "But not today. Not today, please. I don't feel good."

"Alright, Uncle Sophal, not today, but can we pray together."

I was confused and needed clarification. I didn't understand what that meant.

"Why do I need to pray?" I asked him.

"That's the key to understanding the Book of Mormon," Artie explained. "You need to ask God if it is true."

"I don't understand," I told him.

Then, Artie clasped my hands, bowed his head, and prayed with me. He asked God to open my eyes and mind and help me understand what I would read in the Book of Mormon. As he prayed, I trembled. I could feel myself shaking. Artie explained that I was feeling the Spirit of God—the Holy Ghost.

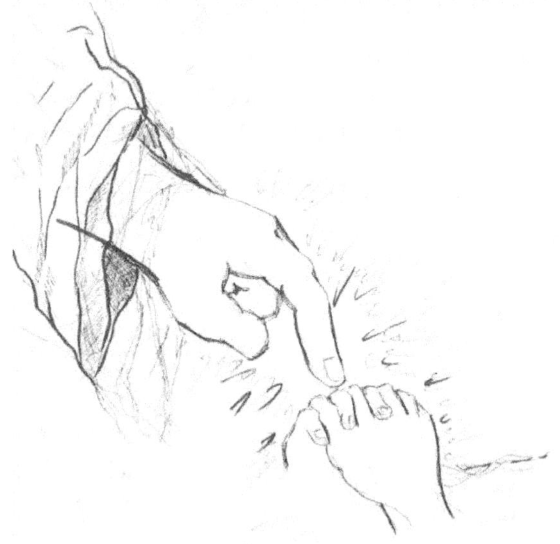

He continued to urge me to give the Book of Mormon a chance, emphasizing how meaningful it could be for me, especially the story about Nephi. He told me to pray and to ask God if the Book of Mormon is true.

## 16.   Healing Waters

Eventually, after about two weeks, I read a few chapters from First Nephi. Still, I didn't understand a lot of what I was reading. Artie reminded me to pray before I read and promised that God would open my mind.

I wanted to pray but didn't know how. I told Artie, "I don't know what to say."

Again, Artie gave me the key.

"Ask to know if the Book of Mormon is true. It's that simple. Just say, 'Heavenly Father, show me if this book is true.'"

His advice gave me hope and clarity. With this key, I felt ready to seek understanding through prayer. I began to read again where God commanded Nephi to build a ship and to cross the ocean. I read with great interest how his brothers were angry with him and beat him and tied him up until a great storm came. I realized that I was crying now as I read Nephi's story.

I was astonished as I read, and memories flooded back about the three ships we had used to escape Cambodia. The vivid recollection of those desperate days gripped me.

The hatred our brothers held for us was unthinkable. They were our people, yet they brutally murdered everyone on P113. Young people and older people alike—there was no distinction.

Their resentment had escalated to such an extent that it consumed them completely. It didn't matter if you were a neighbor or even family; their hatred knew no bounds. They slaughtered all two hundred souls without hesitation.

It's hard to fathom how deep the hatred among fellow citizens ran. We shared the same land, language, and history, yet they turned against us with such ferocity. This memory haunts me profoundly. Laman and

Lemuel had this same murderous spirit toward their father, Lehi, and their brother, Nephi.

The storms we faced at sea were never as fierce as the one Nephi describes, but they were terrifying, nonetheless. Thunder and lightning tormented us often during our journey to the Philippines. The noise was deafening, and each flash of lightning felt like a threat aimed directly at us.

Our two remaining ships moved low in the water, weighed down by the crowds of frightened people who had fled with us. Every gust of wind made us fear for our safety. We clung to whatever hope we could muster, but seeing dark clouds on the horizon often filled us with dread. Our survival seemed uncertain with every passing storm.

Each day felt like a battle against nature itself. Survival wasn't just about making it through the storm but about keeping our spirits alive amidst the raging elements. With little room to move, we prayed to see the light at the end of this challenging journey.

As I read these chapters in Nephi, tears rose in my eyes. I was struck by the profound realization that God's hand had guided me to safety and a promised land. I was taken aback by everything I had endured and survived. The fear that once overwhelmed me during my escape from Cambodia now felt like a distant memory. An immense sense of gratitude has replaced it.

Reflecting on my life, I'm amazed by all I've survived. Each hardship faced seems part of a grand design, leading to this moment of overwhelming thankfulness. God's grace and benevolence in preserving me still astounds me today. He protected me from the fury of the ocean and the dark bitterness within people's hearts. This journey out of turmoil was nothing short of miraculous.

As I closed those chapters of Nephi, a profound realization dawned on me. Nephi was, in many ways, like me—a refugee fleeing his homeland under the threat of death from his own people. He braved the uncertainty and peril of crossing a vast ocean for safety and a new beginning. His unwavering faith guided him to a land of great promise.

Reflecting on this, I felt a deep connection with Nephi's journey. Like him, I've had to leave behind everything familiar and dear to escape danger. My path has been fraught with challenges and fears about the unknown future. The account of Lehi and his family inspired my life and my art—I have painted Lehi's journey across the ocean based in part on my own journey of suffering and torment.

As I closed those sacred pages, it struck me: the story of Nephi is my story, too. Our faith led us to places we hoped would bring peace and opportunity. This shared narrative gives me strength and hope for what lies ahead.

The next time I met with Artie Johnson, he asked if I had been reading the Book of Mormon. His inquiry was warm and genuine, reflecting his deep interest in my spiritual journey. I nodded and smiled, eager to share my latest experience.

My voice trembled slightly as I recounted how those scriptures spoke directly to my heart. Emotions welled within me, making it hard to describe their full impact. Artie listened intently, his eyes shining with understanding. He understood exactly what I was expressing. This shared moment of connection deepened our friendship and added new meaning to my spiritual exploration.

"Well, Uncle Sophal," Artie told me. "Then you need to be baptized."

"Baptized?" I questioned. "Why do I need to be baptized?"

Artie looked at me with a knowing smile.

"Because if you believe the Book of Mormon, then you believe that Jesus Christ is the Son of God. You need to be baptized to take on the name of Jesus Christ and to repent for sins from your past," he explained.

"I already repented," I told him. "I take care of my family."

"It's more than that, Uncle Sophal," he told me. "When you left Cambodia, it was more than just crossing an ocean. It was a journey that took you around the entire world. Every step of the way, you were supported by the hand of God, guiding you through uncharted territories.

"Your heavenly Father upheld you during this intense voyage, providing comfort and strength. You saw His grace in moments of uncertainty and felt His presence in times of fear. Divine intervention played a critical role in your safe passage. In every obstacle, a touch of God's love guided you forward. You must recognize that God's hand carried you where mere human strength could not, Sophal."

I reflected momentarily on my conversation with my friend. His words echoed in my mind. At first, I was reluctant to accept his perspective, but the more I pondered, the clearer it became. The realization finally dawned on me—he was right.

"I'm sorry," I told him. "You are right. I need to be baptized."

It wasn't a difficult choice, but it had an element of sorrow. Having been raised to view Buddha as a god and then realizing that he was just an average person made me feel sad. I still respect him. I honor him because he was a good person, much like a prophet, and he taught moral principles. But I now recognize that there is only one God, our Father in heaven and that Jesus is His Only Begotten Son.

Two months later, about six months after meeting Artie Johnson, I was baptized a member of the Church of Jesus Christ of Latter-day Saints. The day I was baptized, I experienced a profound transformation. As soon as the water touched my skin, I felt an immediate and tangible shift within me. My body felt lighter, almost as if a weight had been lifted. The heaviness that had once clung to me so tightly evaporated.

I was enveloped in an overwhelming sense of peace. It wasn't just calmness but a deep-seated tranquility that washed over my entire being. Joy filled my heart to the brim, radiating outward with each breath I took.

Most strikingly, I felt clean in a way I'd never felt before—physically, spiritually, and emotionally. This newfound cleanliness permeated every cell of my body. It was as if all the impurities and doubts had been rinsed away. I had been cleansed by the healing waters of baptism.

At that moment, standing there drenched yet renewed, I realized that this change was not temporary. It marked the beginning of a new life filled with hope and possibilities.

# 17.    I Had a Dream

After my baptism, I went home. I felt different. My heart was light as if the water had washed away the remnants of my past and lingering fears. The sun's warmth seemed more vivid, and the world around me felt infused with a new vibrancy.

It's hard to explain. I knew I was Sophal, and I knew my hands and body, but my hands and body felt different somehow. I felt lighter than I have ever felt in my life.

That night, after I fell asleep, I had a dream. I was walking along a street. The street was straight and lined with trees on both sides, and it seemed to be in the air, not exactly in the sky but above the Earth. It floated somewhere in between.

As I walked on, I saw a lady taller than me, dressed all in white. Everything she wore was pure white. She smiled at me and said,

"Welcome home, Sophal. Welcome home."

She turned to go, then looked back at me.

"Look at the sign, Sophal," she told me. "Do you see what it says?"

Then, I saw a banner stretching from left to right. It was in English, and it read, "Welcome Home."

When I woke, my heart was beating hard and fast.

* * * * *

When I explained my decision to join the church to my parents, they were unhappy. They thought I had forgotten my Cambodian traditions and upbringing. I shared with them my feelings about the Book of Mormon and our miraculous journey to our own promised land.

I asked my parents what would have happened to us if we hadn't left Cambodia when we did. The chaos and violence of the Khmer Rouge takeover could have engulfed us. As members of the military, we would have been killed. Others might have been forced into labor camps, struggling for survival under brutal conditions.

What if our ship had returned to Phnom Penh like P113? We might have faced brutal murder upon arrival. Our fate could have mirrored many others who disappeared during that dark period.

And what if a storm had sunk our ship? The sea could have claimed us, ending our journey abruptly and tragically. We would never know the safety or hope of a new beginning. Each possibility, I told them, paints a grim picture, making our escape feel even more miraculous.

My parents remained quiet.

We had lost so many of our friends and family. The Khmer Rouge had slaughtered aunts and uncles, nieces, nephews, and cousins. I was sure my brother, Sophon, had also been killed.

And I would have been killed, too.

# 18.   Lost Brother

"I'm not going," Sophon said with a surprising certainty in his voice. I looked at him incredulously.

"What do you mean, 'You're not going?' You must go," I told him. "The Khmer Rouge are taking over Phnom Penh. You must come with us."

His face hardened into an expression of fierce determination that betrayed no trace of fear.

"No, Sophal, I have decided to stay in Cambodia," he explained. "I'm going to protect the bay. That's my job."

His words hit me like a punch in the stomach. I knew my brother would be facing certain death if he remained in Cambodia.

"If you stay, you'll be killed," I warned him.

"You get our family to safety. Get Mom and Dad and our sisters out of here. Don't worry about me."

That was the last conversation I had with my brother.

* * * * *

After Phnom Penh fell into the hands of the Khmer Rouge, people were ordered out of their homes and into the streets. The Communist Regime directed all military personnel to stand on one side of the street, as regular citizens were commanded to stand on the opposite side. There were about seven hundred soldiers of varying ranks still in the city.

That evening, the Khmer Rouge army ordered the former military personnel into the back of several large trucks. They drove the trucks into the mountainous jungle, backed them up to near-vertical cliffs, and then dumped the unsuspecting former military over the edge. Anyone attempting to prevent themselves from falling by hanging onto the truck was either shot or had his hands chopped off with a machete. My brother, Sophon, was among them.

* * * * *

At first, Sophon was only aware of a dampness against his skin. The drip of morning dew brought him back into consciousness. Searing pain was the next sensation that awakened him to a full recollection of what had happened the night before. The fall from the truck had left Sophon unconscious at the base of the cliff for the night. His body ached all over, but it appeared that he was otherwise uninjured.

The dead lay all around him, and he could hear the faint groanings of a few fellow soldiers who had survived. They suffered lacerations, broken bones, and other injuries. If their wounds didn't kill them, Sophon felt sure the venomous snakes that threaded these jungle floors soon would. One thing was sure: Sophon knew he needed to find his way out of that jungle death hole. He stood up and began limping back toward Phnom Penh.

Outside the city, he removed his uniform, knowing that he would be shot if he was seen wearing it. Shortly after, as he approached the town, several soldiers from the Khmer Rouge spotted him. They ordered him to stop.

They grilled him for several minutes, demanding to know who he was, where he had come from, and what he was doing wandering without any clothes. He gave them his name and told them he was a musician—a drummer—and had been out walking. The soldiers then took Sophon to a labor camp where he was held prisoner and forced to work for the Khmer Rouge.

At the time of Phnom Penh's fall, the Cambodian economy was at a standstill due to the devastation of the civil war and the bombing of *Operation Menu*. The Khmer Rouge intensified the paralysis by shutting down banks, sometimes physically destroying them. They abolished the national currency and free markets and confiscated private property.

The members of the forced labor camps were fed a spoonful of rice per day. If they were fortunate enough to scavenge a bit of bok choy, potato, or some other vegetable, they would cook it together with the rice. Anyone caught stealing food would be beaten to death. The Khmer Rouge wasn't willing to waste a bullet on a vegetable thief.

As the Khmer Rouge lengthened its rule, mismanagement created increasing shortages of food, drugs, and primary medical care. After murdering many of its doctors, countless Cambodians succumbed to preventable and curable diseases. Between 500,000 and 1.5 million lives were lost during these four years due to famine.

Overworked and underfed, Sophon would often lick the asphalt on the road, hoping to get some salt into his system. Returning from his labors one evening, Sophon was stopped by three Khmer Rouge soldiers. They ordered him to climb a nearby coconut tree and drop a coconut down to them.

"If you refuse," they told Sophon, "you will be shot."

Exhausted and malnourished, Sophon had no choice but to climb the tree. The rough bark scraped against his bare skin as he attempted to ascend the tall coconut tree. The effort proved to be more than he could endure. Halfway up the tree, too weak to continue, Sophon fell to the ground, his skin tearing as it scraped against the tree's bark. He hit the hard ground and collapsed unconscious once again.

Scratched, bleeding, and unresponsive, lying on the side of the road beneath the coconut tree, Sophon was left for dead by the Khmer Rouge soldiers. He regained consciousness the following morning and was returning to the labor camp when the same three soldiers spotted him.

"You're still alive?" they asked.

Sophon nodded.

"Good. Get your tools and get to work," they ordered.

Sophon obeyed.

For nearly four years, the Khmer Rouge perpetrated one of the greatest crimes of the 20th century. Almost two million people died under the rule of the militant Communist movement, with its imposed ruthless agenda of forced labor, thought control, and mass execution. The goal was to transform Cambodia into a classless agrarian utopia. The result was the wholesale destruction of an ancient society and a horrifying new term for the world to confront: "the killing fields."

* * * * *

Shortly after my baptism, four or five years after I left Cambodia, I received a visit from the president of the Cambodia Association in Sandy.

"Sophal, I have good news!" he told me. "They have found your brother!"

I was ecstatic. For so long, I had assumed the Khmer Rouge had murdered my brother. My heart swelled with joy to learn that Sophon was still alive.

The President of the Association gave me a letter that I needed to sign and return to immigration, along with several other forms that needed to be filled out. The letter also contained a photograph of my brother for verification.

I immediately wrote to my brother and sent him money, clothes, and medicine. The first letter I sent was by airmail. It took a week to arrive and cost nearly sixty dollars to mail. I also called my sponsor back in Virginia to ask if he had heard the news about my brother. He said he had also received a copy of the letter and was extremely happy for me.

When I left Cambodia, my brother was a single man working in the Cambodian Royal Navy. He was now married and had a family. He lived in the countryside, about twenty miles outside Phnom Penh, and worked as a teacher.

I had heard that the church had begun sending missionaries to Cambodia, and I told my brother that I had joined the Church of Jesus Christ of Latter-day Saints. At that time, there were only two branches of the church in Cambodia, one of which was in Phnom Penh.

"I have seen them," Sophon told me. "Young American boys with white shirts knocking on doors. Is that the church you joined?"

"Yes. That's the one," I told Sophon. "You need to go into town and search for the missionaries."

Sophon walked twenty miles into Phnom Penh to find the church. The branch president was skeptical about Sophon's claim that he had a brother in Sandy, Utah, who was a member of the church. Cambodia was still experiencing immense political unrest and crime, and the Branch President needed assurance that Sophon was telling the truth. A quick computer check revealed that Sophon did, in fact, have a brother living in Sandy, Utah, who was a member of the Church of Jesus Christ of Latter-day Saints.

Week after week, Sophon walked twenty miles into Phnom Penh to attend church and learn about the restored gospel. Because of the distance he had to travel on foot, he would stay overnight in the city with one of my mom's relatives.

My brother eventually moved to Phnom Penh and was baptized into the Church of Jesus Christ of Latter-day Saints. At the time of this writing, he serves as a Bishop for the church.

# 19.  Epilogue

Looking back over my life, I am filled with a sense of awe and disbelief that I am still alive. I had been spared from government police, landmines, snake bites, and bombed military vessels. I watched my friends die right in my arms, and yet I remain alive. After all these years, it is still difficult to fathom surviving amid such overwhelming tragedies.

There have been moments of sheer terror where the odds were against me, yet God intervened. Each close call, each unforeseeable tragedy, has woven a tapestry of lessons learned and wisdom gained, all under the guiding light of faith.

My life has swayed like autumn leaves caught in a storm; loss has painted shades of gray across a bright future full of promise. Yet amidst all this chaos, there is a profound beauty—a recognition that every moment holds a deep and meaningful significance, no matter how fragile.

There is a sense of beauty within survival itself—the ability to look back at the winding road behind me and see struggles and triumphs etched along the way. Each tragedy along that path nurtured growth—each unpredictable disaster ripe with possibility.

Reflecting on these chapters reminds me how precious time truly is; it compels me to savor each day I'm given rather than take it for granted. The memories linger like shadows, haunting yet distant. Each moment recalls the loss—names and faces that flash before my eyes like a flickering film, reminding me of life interrupted. I often reflect on resilience—what it means to rise from the ashes when everything around you seems charred beyond recognition.

Then there are days when hope peeks through the cracks—a soft glow illuminating the dark corners where despair had flourished for so long. This flicker fuels my spirit, urging me to cherish life's fleeting moments.

As seasons change and years pass, I've learned that healing is not linear—it twists and turns unpredictably. Setbacks that feel insurmountable are followed by more profound strides toward clarity. While scars may remain etched upon my heart, they tell stories of survival.

In this intricate tapestry woven with threads of both joy and pain, I am reminded that we can honor our losses while embracing life fully—a delicate balance between remembering what was lost and cherishing what's left after enduring hardships.

Every morning, I wake up with a heart full of gratitude to my Heavenly Father for sparing my life and leading me to the restored Gospel of Jesus Christ. This belief system emphasizes the teachings and principles of Jesus Christ as revealed to the Prophet Joseph Smith. This faith has become my guiding light, offering me guidance and strength and helping me navigate the challenges of each day.

In moments of uncertainty or doubt, the scriptures become a lifeline infused with comfort and reassurance. I often reflect on the sacrifices made by Lehi and Nephi and their families, and their faith inspires me to deepen my relationship with God. The story of

Nephi's unwavering faith in building a ship despite his lack of experience always reminds me to trust in God's plan. Through trials that test my resolve and triumphs that bring joy, this divine connection fuels my spirit. Each moment is an opportunity for growth as I strive to live a life reflective of His grace.

Each day, I reflect on the countless blessings surrounding me—my family, friends, and even the challenges that have shaped me into the person I have become. When trials arise, I hold the assurance that God is always by my side. Prayer becomes an avenue for intimate conversation filled with trust in His infinite wisdom. I find solace in prayer, lifting my thoughts toward Him, seeking knowledge and understanding as I strive to align my actions with His will.

I express gratitude for another day lived in His light. Reflecting on each moment spent living out lessons learned from my devastating personal experiences grounds me firmly in faith and hope as tomorrow approaches—a fresh canvas and divine inspiration guiding each brushstroke.

www.ingramcontent.com/pod-product-compliance
Lightning Source LLC
Chambersburg PA
CBHW050516160726
48003CB00001B/332